NOT
KNOWING
WHERE

P U B L I S H E R S
BOX 3566 • GRAND RAPIDS. MI 49501

*PUBLISHING BOOKS THAT FEED
THE SOUL WITH THE WORD OF GOD.*

NOT KNOWING WHERE

OSWALD CHAMBERS

Published through special arrangement with the
Oswald Chambers Publications Association

To our Mother
whose interest in the sending forth of my husband's messages has
been an unfailing source of inspiration.—B.C.

Father, the narrow path
   To that far country show;
And in the steps of Abraham's faith
   Enable me to go.
A cheerful sojourner
   Where'er Thou bidst me roam,
Till, guided by Thy Spirit here,
   I reach my heavenly home.

CONTENTS

Publisher's Foreword

Few Christian writers in this century seem to have tapped the spiritual realities of our biblical faith as has Oswald Chambers. Known for his bestselling devotional book, *My Utmost for His Highest,* his writings have been compiled into a library of more than thirty volumes, most of which are unknown even to those who have read *My Utmost.* Because we believe the Christian community needs to rediscover Chambers, Discovery House Publishers is committed to reprinting new, updated editions of the Oswald Chambers Library. The third volume in the series is this study of the book of Genesis, *Not Knowing Where,* with its focus on the life of Abraham. The present edition is an amalgamation of two previously published Chambers' works, *Our Portrait in Genesis* and *Not Knowing Whither,* with an additional chapter on the Tower of Babel by Arthur Neil.

Believers need to hear again from this great devotional writer, to learn the art of biblical meditation, to reflect on the Word of God as taught by the Spirit of God, to know the mind of Christ, and to "appraise all things" from His divine perspective (1 Cor. 2:9–16).

The author's style is brief and meditative. His work must be read slowly and contemplatively so that his words can be assimilated into one's own thought and behavior.

As a theologian Chambers is noncritical, dealing with truth as it affects us personally rather than coming to the teachings of Scripture dogmatically and critically. He uses a doctrinal vocabulary, which, at times, is general rather than systematically precise, reflecting the less technical posture of evangelical believers in the early years of this century.

We, the publishers, commend *Not Knowing Where* to you, trusting that by reading it you will discover afresh the reality of faith at work, making the Father known to you, the Son real to you, the Spirit alive to you, and the Word rewarding to you.

The Publisher

Foreword to the New Edition

In amalgamating these gems from Genesis in this new edition, our prayer is that these precious truths from the anointed and incisive ministry of Oswald Chambers at the beginning of this century, with its relevant teaching in depth, will come with fresh vitality to the church in time for the great spiritual need at the end of the century.

Arthur Neil
O.C.P.A.

Foreword

Now these things were our examples (1 Corinthians 10:6).

We know nothing of the beginning of life on this planet unless we accept the biblical record. When we accept these early stories as a true account of individual lives, we can learn much about God's dealings with men and women in every age. We see flashes of light that can jolt a modern wrongdoer, and we see divine mercy as it persists with perverse and misguided men.

Oswald Chambers brings out the moral significance of human conduct. He shows how sin has intruded into human affairs, and he reveals God's counter-move against sin and the satanic power behind the scenes. "Now these things were our examples," wrote the apostle Paul in reference to some Old Testament incidents. In Cain and Abel, Noah, and Abraham we have examples of such things as the subtle working of sin in the unregenerate human heart, the craftiness and insincerity between men, and the law of retribution or due recompense.

In this book, still so relevant for our day, we see the deep things of God, especially as they bear on the deep things of humanity. Above all, we hear of the God of all grace, who gave His Son to be a propitiation for our sins, "and not for ours only, but also for the whole world."

Here, in this volume, are studies of Abraham, that great pioneer of the life of faith. In them we see faith's reactions to God's call, to clashing circumstances, to the claims of companions, and to the terrific cost of God's friendship. These studies link up in a wonderful way the experience of grace under the new covenant with the eternal purpose of God made plain under the old covenant. Abraham is studied as a forerunner of modern saints in their faith-walk.

The book is replete with spiritual wisdom. The very chapter titles betray that touch of genius which sparkles in the pages. If great books are the lifeblood of the world's master spirits, then this book is the lifeblood of one who by grace was brought to the fullness of the stature of Christ. These studies make possible a term of guided reading on this outstanding example of the walk of faith in this world of men.

I thank God for this gallery of portraits in Genesis, and for the Spirit's illumination through the instructed and clear-seeing mind of Oswald Chambers.

David Lambert

Genesis 1–2

Beginnings

In the beginning God (1:1).

"I am the Alpha and the Omega, *the* beginning and *the* End," says the Lord, "who is and who was and who is to come, the Almighty" (Revelation 1:8).

The Bible never argues or debates; it states revelation facts. Our understanding of these facts depends on a relationship of faith, not on intellectual curiosity, and our perception of these Bible truths is granted by the Holy Spirit. The remarkable thing about the Holy Spirit's illumination is that it commends itself as being the true interpretation to every child of God who is in the light.

Science (knowledge systematized) is man's intellectual effort to explain established facts that intelligent people accept; it is the attempt to arrange these facts into some kind of unity that will not contradict the fundamental way we are made. When we are born again, however, we come in contact with another domain of facts—that is, biblical revelation—and there must be an "at-one-ment" made between the two domains. We are apt to accept scientific truth readily and to be skeptical about revelations made by the Holy Spirit. Our tendency is to put truth into a creed. But truth is a Person. "I am the truth," Jesus said.

The earth was without form, and void (1:2).

By faith we understand that the worlds were framed by the word of God, so that the things which are seen were not made of things which are visible (Hebrews 11:3).

Chaos—the state of matter before it was reduced to order by the Creator—is not to be regarded necessarily as divine judgment but as the foundation of cosmos, like a painter's palette where he mixes his colors: the artist sees in it what we cannot. The constructed world we see today is not the created world of God, for it has had a formation put upon it which is not of God. We don't need to reform the basis; we need to remove what has been erected on it. If we build our lives on things God did not form, He will have to destroy them—shake them back into chaos.

When a man sees the light of God for the first time, it produces conviction of sin, and he cries out, "Depart from me; for I am a sinful man, O Lord." When the Holy Spirit comes into a man, "his beauty is consumed away"; the perfectly ordered completeness of his whole nature is broken up. Then the Holy Spirit, brooding over the resulting chaos, brings a word of God, and as that word is received and obeyed, a new life is formed.

"And the spirit of God was hovering over the face of the waters. Then God said, 'Let there be light'; and there was light" (1:3). God's word creates by its own power. God speaks and His word performs what He sends it to accomplish (see Isaiah 55:11).

"And God saw the light, that it was good" (1:4). God's creation satisfies Him, and when we come to know God by His Spirit, we are as delighted with His creation as He is Himself. A child enjoys all that God has created; everything is wonderful to him.

In the beginning God's word created the world, and the witness of the word satisfied God. So too the work of Christ in a disciple witnesses to Him. Our value to God is that when we obey His spoken word we become in reality the idea He had before He spoke. God's word expressed in us becomes its own witness to God.

God's word is clear and emphatic, and when we first hear it we are full of joy; but that word doesn't give God satisfaction until it becomes real in us. The fanatic mistakes the vision the word brings for its actual expression. But we must be prepared to put God's word into its rightful place, into the matter of "me," where it will bring forth God's idea. It is not our faith laying hold of the word, but the life in the word laying hold of us. Strictly speaking, no seed contains in itself the mature plant. The forces acting outside it, as well as its own inherent life, determine what it will be.

> Then God saw everything that He had made, and indeed it was very good. . . . Then God blessed the seventh day and sanctified it, because in it He rested from all His work which God had created and made (1:31; 2:3).

Six days God labored, *thinking* Creation, until it was as He thought. On the seventh day He rested, not from fatigue but because that work was finished.

> And the LORD God formed man *of* the dust of the ground (2:7).

> The first man *was* of the earth, *made* of dust (1 Corinthians 15:47).

These verses refer to our fundamental nature, not to the doctrine of sin. We are made of two things: dust and divinity. That we are made of the dust of the ground is our glory, not our shame, because in it we are to manifest the image of God. Because we are "of the earth, *made* of dust," we are apt to think of it as our humiliation, but it is not so; it is the very thing God's word makes most of. A doctrine that has gotten an octopus-like hold on Christianity is the belief that sin is in matter and that, therefore, as long as there is any "matter" about us there must be sin in us. If sin were in matter, it would be untrue to say that Jesus Christ was "without sin" because He became flesh and blood. Sin does not belong to human nature as God designed it. Therefore, to speak about sin as being eradicated or rooted up is nonsense; it never was planted.

We have no business saying, "In Christ I am all right, but in myself I am all wrong." We must live so that everything related to our physical lives is in harmony with the life of the Son of God in us.

The originator and maintainer of the new life imparted to us is Christ Himself, and His words reveal His fathomless conception of that life: "He who eats My flesh and drinks My blood abides in Me, and I in him" (John 6:56). Before we were redeemed, the disposition of self-will ruled our lives: "You touch me, and I'll hit you." Or, "You touch me, and I'll boil with passion." But Jesus says we should let the very corpuscles of our blood, every nerve and cell of our flesh, exhibit the new life that has been created in us.

"Do you not know that your body is the temple of the Holy Spirit who is in you?" This bodily temple of the Holy Spirit is a fleshly temple, not a spiritual one. The whole meaning of being born again and becoming identified with the death of Christ is that His life might be manifested in our mortal flesh. When we are born from above, the life of the Son of God is born in us, and the perfection of that life enables us not only to know what the will of God is, but to carry out His will in our natural human life.

Genesis 3

Temptation in Paradise

And they heard the sound of the LORD God walking in the garden in the cool of the day, and Adam and his wife hid themselves from the presence of the LORD God among the trees of the garden (3:8).

There is something inconceivable to us in Adam's and Eve's relationship to God, for they saw God as simply as we see one another. Until Adam and Eve fell, they were one with God in communion. When they fell, however, Adam and Eve suddenly became *interested in* God because they were afraid of Him—so afraid that they hid themselves from Him.

Sin finds us severed from God and interested in anything we can be told about Him. Consequently there is an element of fear in our interest. When we become children of God, there is no fear. As long as a child has not done wrong, he enjoys perfect freedom and confidence toward his parents; but let him disobey, and suddenly he is concerned about where his parents are and what they are thinking. He is interested in the ones he has disobeyed—interested out of fear. Conscious piety springs from being interested in God: "Am I right with God?" Those who are right with Him are so one with Him that they are unconscious of it. Their relationship is deeper than conscious-ness because they are being disposed by the very nature of God.

Sin is not part of human nature as God designed it. The Bible looks on sin, not as a disease, but as red-handed rebellion against the Creator. The essence of sin is: "I won't allow anybody to boss me except myself," and it may manifest itself in a morally good person as well as in a morally bad one. Sin is not about morality or immorality; it has to do with my claim to my right to myself, a deliberate and emphatic independence of God, though I cover it with a veneer of Christian phraseology. If I allow this spirit to get back into me, I become the embodiment of heaven and hell in conflict.

> And the LORD God commanded the man, saying, "Of every tree of the garden you may freely eat: but of the tree of the knowledge of good and evil you shall not eat, for in the day that you eat of it you shall surely die." . . . Then the serpent said to the woman, "You will not surely die" (2:16–17; 3:4).

Eve finds that what Satan told her is true: death does not strike them all at once. However, secretly, underneath everything, death has begun. Something similar happens to us today. We transgress a law of God and expect an experience akin to death; yet exactly the opposite happens. We feel enlarged, more broad-minded, more tolerant to evil. But what we are is powerless. Instead of instigating us to action, knowledge of good and evil paralyzes.

> For the wages of sin is death (Romans 6:23).

We become subject to death not because we are finite beings, but because of sin. Whenever we touch sin, death is the inevitable result; it is the way God has constituted us. When we are "alive" in sin, we are "dead" to God. "And you *He made alive,* who were dead in trespasses and sins" (Ephesians 2:1). Death was not in God's purpose for man, but "through one man . . . death spread to all men, because all sinned" (Romans 5:12). Thus, every human being inherits the *disposition* of sin.

"You cannot see My face; for no man shall see Me, and live," God told Moses (Exodus 33:20). And yet we do see God and live—but only by going through death. When we are born again, we are also experiencing death. For to be born again we must die—die to our claim to our right to ourselves—and receive the gift of eternal life, which is "the gift of God . . . in Jesus Christ our Lord" (Romans 6:23).

> Then the man said, "The woman whom You gave *to be* with me, she gave me of the tree, and I ate" (3:12).

> The woman said, "The serpent deceived me, and I ate" (3:13).

Adam does not blame himself; neither does Eve blame herself. They both evade the moral truth. (Verbal truth is rarely moral truth.) Adam *admits*, but he does not confess. Rather, he implies that God is to blame for his actions: "You should not have put me in a position where I could disobey," he complains. "I don't deny I did wrong, but remember the extenuating circumstances. You shouldn't be so stern and holy." This aversion to God's holiness is the first manifestation of the spirit of anarchy. The diabolical nature of sin hates God, because when it comes face to face with the holiness of God it knows there is no escape. Consequently there is nothing the natural heart of man hates like a holy God.

If only God would not be as holy as our conscience tells us He is. This is our mixed-up certainty: we know we are not right with God and we don't want to be—and yet we do. We will do anything rather than take the responsibility on ourselves for having done wrong; or if we do accept the responsibility, we defy God to readjust us. One response is as bad as the other. Either we refuse to say we have sinned, or we admit we have sinned and refuse to let God save us. We won't allow God to have the last word.

"If we *confess* our sins," says the apostle John. Whenever conviction of sin comes, we must pull it out into the light and confess it; for when we realize the shame of sin and accept God's forgiveness, an inwrought energy replaces the energy which went out in the sin. That energy is recovered in "the fruits of repentance."

> So the LORD God said to the serpent: ". . . I will put enmity between you and the woman, and between your seed and her Seed" (3:14, 15).

Man must deal with Satan because man is responsible for his introduction into this world. That is why God became Incarnate. If He wanted to, God could banish Satan in two seconds. But it is man who, through the redemption, is to overcome Satan and do that which will exhibit the perfect fulfillment of His prophecy regarding the serpent. And it is through Jesus Christ, the last Adam, who took on Himself our human form, that Satan is ultimately to be overcome. "And the God of peace will crush Satan under your feet shortly" (Romans 16:20). As we come to God by the way back provided by Jesus Christ, He will restore everything that Satan and sin have marred.

Genesis 4

Message of God on Sin

And it came to pass, when they were in the field, that Cain rose up against Abel his brother, and killed him (4:8).

No man can murder his brother who has not first murdered God in himself. Cain's crime was much deeper and greater than the murder of his brother; it was the rebellion of his whole nature against God.

Sin at the Door (4:1–10)

In verses 6 and 7 we see God doing for Cain what He did for Adam and Eve: giving him a divine opportunity for repentance. Notice I say repentance, not remorse. Remorse is never repentance; remorse is the rebellion of man's own pride which will not agree with God's judgment on sin but accuses God because He has made His laws too stern and holy. Adam and Eve acknowledged their sin, but they never confessed it. Their son Cain evaded even acknowledgment. First he lied to God; then he became scornful of God: "Am I my brother's keeper?"

In Adam and Eve sin revealed itself as envy of God; in Cain it advanced to envy of his brother. "And the LORD respected Abel and his offering, but He did not respect Cain and his offering. And Cain was very angry, and his countenance fell" (4:4–5). Personal vindictive rage is the spirit of murder, and that is what drove Cain to murder his brother Abel. "And why did he murder him? Because his works were evil and his brother's righteous. . . . Whoever hates his brother is a murderer" (1 John 3:12, 15).

> And He said, "What have you done? The voice of your brother's blood cries out to Me from the ground" (4:10).

Murder may be done in a hundred and one ways. Think of the number of voices that cry out to God today! The cry of every murdered innocent, every victim in our civilized world, rings in the ear of God. And in this sense the blood of Abel still speaks and will never be silenced.

The Solitariness of Guilt (4:11–12)

> "So now you *are* cursed from the earth, which has opened its mouth to receive your brother's blood from your hand. When you till the ground, it shall no longer yield its strength to you. A fugitive and a vagabond you shall be on the earth" (4:11–12).

Beware of speaking of *reaction* when God says *retribution*. The man who has done wrong has such a guilty conscience that he imagines everything is against him. Everything is against him, of course, for God is against him. In that sense, every bit of earth is against him; he stands absolutely alone. Nothing associates itself with the sinner except his own sin. Once sin enters in, he is out of gear with God morally and with the universe physically.

> And Cain said to the LORD, "My punishment *is* greater than I can bear! Surely You have driven me out this day from the face of the ground; I shall be hidden from Your face; I shall be a fugitive and a vagabond on the earth" (4:13–14).

Cain takes God's punishment, which is actually His mercy, and perverts it into a penal decree making it impossible for him to come back. He wraps himself in the garment of despair and spits back accusations against God: "See what You have done to me! You have cut me off from everything I care about."

When our wrongdoing results in God's punishment, we are all prone to a similar attitude: "Oh, well, it's no use trying to do any better. God has sent me from His presence, and I can't get back, so I can do as I like now." Beware of this kind of sulky, self-pitying, despairing complaint, which is a threatening accusation against God. The door is always open to God until we shut it. God never shuts it; we shut it. Then we lose the key and say, "It's all over; whatever I do now, God is entirely to blame."

Never disassociate yourself from anything any human being has ever done, saying, "I don't know how anyone could do that. I could never do such a thing." That is the delusion of a moral lunatic. God will give you such a knowledge of yourself that you will know, in humility before Him, how the vilest crime could be committed. You won't say, "But I could never do that"; you could. Any human being is capable of doing what other human beings have done. When you see a criminal and feel instantly, "How horrible and vile that person is," it is a sure sign that the Lord is not in you. When He is in you, you feel not only the vileness of the crime, but say of yourself, "But for God, I am that, and much worse." This is no pious phrase to be dashed off glibly; it is the awe-ful reality of our sinful nature.

> Then Cain went out from the presence of the LORD and dwelt in the land of Nod (4:16).

According to the marginal note on this text, Nod means "wandering." Cain had no rest anywhere, for the earth spurned him; therefore he went into the land of Wandering and constructed his own world. Men who have sinned and maintain themselves in their sin cannot endure the world God created; so they must make a world of their own.

And Cain . . . built a city (4:17).

The first civilization was founded by a murderer, and the whole basis of civilized life ever since has been a vast, complicated, gilded-over system of murder. We find it more conducive to human welfare, however, not to murder men outright; instead we do it by a system of competition. It is ingrained in our thinking that competition and rivalry are essential to the carrying on of civilized life; that is why Jesus Christ's statements seem wild and ridiculous. One must be a fool, for example, to believe it possible, or even desirable, to carry out His Sermon on the Mount.

And who is that fool? The person who has been born again and who dares to live out the teaching of Jesus.

The Evolution of Depravity

> Then the LORD saw that the wickedness of man *was* great in the earth, and *that* every intent of the thoughts of his heart *was* only evil continually (6:5).

Depravity means much more than going wrong; it means to be so established in the wrong that one takes real pleasure in it. There is a kind of inspiration in choosing to do wrong, a simplification of life. We no longer have to make excuses, for we are without excuse; we become brazenly fixed in the wrong. This is the characteristic of the Devil.

The revelation the Bible makes is not that men are getting worse, but that men are damnable; consequently they can be saved. The system of things may get worse, but a man can't be worse than damnable. If persistently trying to remove the possibility of damnation, man destroys the possibility of the justice of God, destroys his own manhood, and leaves in its place an evolving animal-life in which God is not necessary.

The Floods of Elemental Sin (6:1–5)

Apart from God, the human heart is depraved ("For out of the heart proceed evil thoughts . . ."; "The heart *is* deceitful above all *things,* and desperately wicked" Matthew 15:19; Jeremiah 17:9). The elemental fountain of depravity is there.

If this depravity is not manifested in consciousness it is either because we refuse to accept Jesus Christ's diagnosis or because we have been saved and sanctified by God's mighty grace.

According to our Lord, these evil imaginings reside deep in the moral character that lies below the conscious, the conscious thought, and the conscious purpose. When God's Spirit comes in and opens our consciousness and understanding to the presence of this deep abyss, the only thing to do is to surrender completely to Him and close that abyss forever. It is entire rightness with Jesus Christ alone that prevents elemental depravity from working in the heart and manifesting itself outwardly in deeds.

If we trust Jesus Christ's diagnosis and hand over the keeping of our heart to Him, we need never know in conscious experience what depravity is; but if we trust in our innocent ignorance we are likely one of these days to turn a corner and find that what He said is true. When the crisis comes and men find that what they took to be their innocent heart is really a sink of iniquity, they are the first to say, "Why didn't God tell us?" "Why were we not warned?"

We have been warned, clearly, in order that we need never go through the terrible experience of living out the "murders, adulteries, fornications, thefts, false witness, blasphemies" that proceed "out of the heart." That is the marvelous mercy of God.

Jesus Christ's teaching never beats about the bush. Our stupidity is that we want to believe only what we are conscious of and not the revelation He has made. Instead of being a sign of good taste, it is a sign of shocking unbelief when men won't face what Jesus Christ has put so plainly—so unmistakably plain, so brutally plain at times—about the human heart.

We must never trust our innocent ignorance when Jesus Christ's statements contradict it. Whenever we choose to disregard God, we are acting out of our depravity. We can never rest on the assumption that "Now I am saved and sanctified, all I choose and think is sure to be right." Not by any means. If our choices and our thinking do not spring from a determined recognition of God, we are depraved, no matter what our spiritual experience has been.

The Foundation of Eternal Salvation (6:6–7)

And the LORD was sorry that He had made man on the earth, and He was grieved in His heart (6:6).

An unemotional love is inconceivable. Love for the good must involve displeasure and grief for the evil. God is not an almighty sultan reigning aloof; He is right in the throes of life, and it is there that emotion shows itself.

Our text says that God was sorry He had created man— some translations use the word "repented" ("it repented the LORD that He had made men"). God does not repent like a man; He repents like God—that is, without change of plan or purpose. "God *is* not a man, that He should lie, nor a son of man, that He should repent. Has He said, and will He not do?" (Numbers 23:19).

If God were to say of any sin, "Oh, well, he didn't mean it. I will let it go," that would be a change in God's purpose. If God overlooked one sin in any of us, He would cease to be God. God remains true to His purpose, and that means condemnation; yet that individual condemnation causes the great God of love and mercy grief and agony. The "repenting" of God does not mean that He will overlook wrong; He cannot. His very love forbids it.

When we are saved by God's almighty grace we realize that we have been delivered completely from what He has condemned—and *that* is salvation. We don't excuse sin any longer, but agree with God's verdict on the cross. At the back of all the condemnation of God put "Calvary."

Genesis 6:8–22

The Call of the Forlorn-Hope

But Noah found grace in the eyes of the LORD. . . . Noah was a just man, perfect in his generations. Noah walked with God (6:8–9).

Grace is the overflowing, immeasurable favor of God. God cannot withhold; the only thing that keeps back His grace and favor is our sin and perversity.

Noah Found Grace (6:8–10)

One of the first things said about Noah is that he walked with God—what a statement to have in one's biography! To walk with God means to realize perpetually the nature of faith; that is, that it must be tried or it is mere fancy. Faith untried has no character value for the individual. There is nothing akin to faith in the natural world. Defiant pluck and courage are not faith. It is the *trial* of faith that is "much more precious than of gold," and the trial of faith is never without the essentials of temptation. It is doubtful whether any child of God ever gets through the trial of his faith without at some stage being horror-struck: what God does comes as a stinging blow, and he feels the suffering is not deserved. Yet, like Job, he will neither listen to nor tell lies about God.

Spiritual character is only developed as Noah's was—by standing loyal to God's character, no matter what distress the trial of faith brings. The distress and agony Noah experienced was the distress and agony of believing God when everything that was happening contradicted what he knew Him to be; there was nothing to prove that God was just and true and everything to prove the opposite. This was his forlorn-hope.

Forlorn-hope is the best, perhaps the only, refuge for the godly in Time, when all that has been built on the basis of personal faith in God is contradicted by the immediate present and it is the man who does not believe in God who seems to prosper. When we forget the reality of this forlorn-hope, expressed so eloquently in passages such as Psalm 73, we cease to walk with God and only pay court visits to Him. To walk with God means walking apart from godless reliances. There is no such thing as a *venture* of faith, only a determined *walk with God* by faith.

And God Looked (6:11–16)

> So God looked upon the earth, and indeed it was corrupt; for all flesh had corrupted their way on the earth. . . . "and, behold, I will destroy them with the earth" (6:12, 13).

In these verses we see God's long-suffering patience coming to the conclusion that He must let the full effect of His righteousness have its way. It says that He "looked upon the earth," almost as if until now He had looked away, giving man time through the generations of Enoch and Methuselah and Lamech, all men who walked with God. Then suddenly the gaze of judgment. He looks, and there is no reprieve; the sentence is final.

The pronouncement of coming doom contains both judgment and deliverance, for when God destroys the unsaveable, He liberates the saveable. Consequently, judgment days are the great mercy of God because they separate good and evil; they set apart right from wrong.

Salvation is always a judgment inasmuch as it involves some kind of separation: "The Cross condemns men to salvation." We remain indifferent to the Cross until we realize by the conviction of the Spirit of God that there are certain things in us which are damnable. We can always know the kind of disposition we have by the sword God brings against us. We may plead and pray, but He is merciless; He saves us "so as by fire." Once we are willing to agree with God's condemnation in the Cross, God in His infinite mercy saves us by His judgment. It is not judgment inaugurating salvation, but judgment that *is* salvation—with nations and with the human race.

Make Thee an Ark (6:17–22)

"Make yourself an ark. . . . And behold, I Myself am bringing floodwaters on the earth . . . everything that *is* on the earth shall die. But I will establish My covenant with you; and you shall go into the ark" (6:14, 17, 18).

The ark stands as a reminder that nothing *is* until it is. Whenever we say a thing is impossible the reason is twofold: either our prejudices don't wish it to be, or we wish it so much that it seems too wonderful to be possible. Yet God only does the impossible.

In the realm of what is humanly possible, we don't need God; common sense is our god. We don't pray to God; we pray to some edifice of our common sense. It is God who is the architect of salvation; therefore salvation is not a common-sense design. What we have to do is to get inside that salvation.

If we put our faith in any construction of our own—our vows and decisions, our consecration—we are building something for ourselves. Picture Noah sitting down and saying, "God has given me a wonderful plan. I'm going to sit here and watch it happen." If he had done that, the water would have soon been over his head. Instead, it says, "Thus Noah did; according to all that God commanded him" (6:22).

Still, the initiative springs from the mind of almighty God: "And behold, I Myself am bringing. . . ." It is not the natural consequence of cause and effect. And the result was a covenant with the new humanity after the Flood.

The "afterwards" of God is never disconnected from the "before" of His promise, yet it is more than the fulfillment of that promise. By coming into living relationship with Him, the "afterwards" becomes the re-expression of the fulfillment of the "before" of His purpose.

Genesis 7–9

The Dark of Faith

Now the flood was on the earth forty days. . . . and all the high hills under the whole heaven were covered. . . . Only Noah and those who *were* with him in the ark remained *alive*. And the waters prevailed on the earth one hundred and fifty days (7:17, 19, 23, 24).

The ark itself was submerged, except for the top of it; there was not a foothold anywhere. God removed hope from anywhere but Himself. That is a picture of the kingdom of God in this dispensation: it appears to be completely submerged, yet those very things which look as if they were going to smash it are the things God uses to preserve it.

The Express Covenant

Then God remembered Noah (8:1).

This does not mean that God had forgotten Noah; the remembrances of God are sure to those who will put their trust in Him. It is significant to note here that whenever the Bible uses terms such as "repent," "remember," "forsake," "love," in connection with God, their human meaning does not apply. For example, the love of God can only be illustrated by the character of God.

At last, "the waters decreased"; but the "at last" of God is never an anticlimax, and it always exceeds any possible human forecast. Every word God has spoken will be absolutely fulfilled. We must be careful never to compromise over that, even when it seems that a promise has only been partially fulfilled. We must never assume, "Oh, well, I suppose that is all God meant." To climb down from confidence in God's promises is to be disloyal to Him. Beware, though, of inferring that because no good word of God will fail, we personally will necessarily partake in its fulfillment. We assuredly will not unless we have come into vital relationship with God by determined faith.

And he waited yet another seven days, and again he sent the dove out from the ark (8:10).

Here we see the prominent characteristic of Noah: the humility of patience. Patience is not the same as endurance, for the heart of endurance is frequently stoical, whereas the heart of patience is a blazing love that sees intuitively and awaits God's time in perfect confidence. Also, it is impossible to be both patient and proud because pride weakens into lust, and lust is essentially impatient. Noah stands for all time as the embodiment of the patience of hope.

Then God spoke to Noah, saying, "Go out of the ark. . . ."
So Noah went out (8:15, 18).

As Noah went into the ark at the command of God, so at the command of God he goes forth from the ark. Had Noah been a fanatic, when God said, "Go out of the ark," he would have replied, "No. God told me to stay in the ark. So this must be the voice of the Devil." There is always the danger of becoming a fanatical adherent to what God has said instead of adhering to the God who said it. Noah waited for God's time to go out of the ark.

There is a strong lesson for us as we wait for His reappearing. *When* He comes is a matter of indifference. What matters is that we walk with Him as we wait. What matters is that we retain the certainty of the childlike attitude that God knows what He is about. When the Lord does come, it will be as natural as breathing. God never does anything hysterical, and He never produces hysterics.

The Abiding Relationship

> Then God spoke to Noah and to his sons with him, saying: "And as for Me, behold, I establish My covenant with you and with your descendants after you" (9:8).

God does not do certain things without the cooperation of man. We continually ask, "Why doesn't God do the thing instead of waiting for me?" The answer is that He chooses not to do so. It is like the difference between God's order and His permissive will. His permissive will allows the Devil to do his worst and allows me to sin as I choose, until I choose to resist the Devil, quit sinning, and come to God in the right relationship through Jesus Christ. It is God's will that human beings should get into moral relationship with Him, and His covenants are for that purpose. "Why doesn't God save me?" some ask. He has saved them, but they have not entered into relationship with Him. "Why doesn't God do this and that?" they ask. He has done it. But the point is, will we step into covenant relationship with Him?

All the great blessings of God are finished and complete, but they cannot be ours until we enter into relationship with Him on the basis of His covenant. Salvation is not an edict of God; salvation is something wrought out on the human plane through God becoming man. Waiting for God somehow to do something in us so we can trust in this is incarnate unbelief; it means we have no faith in Him. We have to go out of ourselves to enter into the covenant with God, just as God went out of Himself to enter into His covenant with man (Philippians 2:7–8).

It is a question of faith in God, the rarest thing, for we have faith only in our feelings. We don't believe God unless He will give us something in our hands so we can say, "Now I believe." There is no faith in that.

"Look unto Me and be saved," God says. When we have really transacted business with God on the basis of His covenant, there is a complete, overwhelming sense of having been brought into union with Him—without any sense of merit in ourselves or any human ingredient—and the whole thing is transfigured with peace and joy.

Genesis 11:1–9

The Babel of Souls

Now the whole earth had one language and one speech (11:1).

Following the new beginning, after the judgment of the Flood, the people God had saved and restored spoke one language. This common communication was the bond of their union, the main element of their strength and solidarity. However, they used this unity to nurture and further their own selfish desires and plans. Instead of being directed by pure motives and the glory of God in their invention of building with bricks and mortar, they were governed by pride in their consolidated determination to construct a great city and exalted tower. In their corporate pride they wanted to make a name for themselves. Industry, which is divinely ordained, became distorted by their selfish ambition.

The disposition of sin deifies self; it desires independence from God and human gratification. Sin always contradicts the purpose of God, and we see it clearly in the plans of these plain dwellers. Contrary to the divine command to replenish the flood-washed earth (Genesis 8:17; 9:1), they aimed to establish themselves where they were. "Come, let us build ourselves a city, and a tower whose top *is* in the heavens," they said. "Let us make a name for ourselves, lest we be scattered abroad over the face of the whole earth" (11:4). Their action was designed to substitute their own plans for God's declared purpose.

> "Come, let Us go down and there confuse their language, that they may not understand one another's speech." So the LORD scattered them abroad from there over the face of all the earth, and they ceased building the city. Therefore its name is called Babel, because there the LORD confused the language of all the earth; and from there the LORD scattered them abroad over the face of all the earth (11:7–9).

To oppose the revealed will of God is to court disaster, however, for God had to act against their human pride, policy, and purpose. He made His divine inspection, gave His divine indictment, took His divine initiative, and effected His divine dispersion. The Lord overruled their proud rebellion for His own glory.

Although evil may appear to prevail for a time, God's purpose will succeed.

The Unity of Sin

Notice how the whole of Scripture is knit together over the false unity of the human race—the false unity of sin. Every member of the human race has one common point of interest with every other member, and that is self-interest. And the common objective that results from this common element in human nature is a desire to obliterate God. It is quite possible for the human mind to blot God out of its thinking entirely, and to attempt to band the whole human race into a solid atheistic community—a Babel of souls. Here in this chapter we see this first attempt at "community," way back in antiquity.

There is a bond that unites men known as "the body of sin," and it is the mutual inheritance of the human race (see

Romans 5:12). Satan is anxious to keep that bond intact. The body of sin is this tremendous possibility of solid atheism underlying humanity; the share of individual men and women in that body is called "the old man." The united force of sin forms the basis of the power of Satan, and it runs through the veins of all humanity, making it possible for the whole human race to be atheistic.

At its beginning, sin is simply a state of being without God. Sin is not static, however; it gathers energy which inevitably grows into an active offensive against God and marshalls its forces not only to do without God but to act against Him. There is tremendous power behind wrongdoing; it is a supernatural power antagonistic to God—an oracle of evil (see Ephesians 6:12; 1 John 5:19).

The Unity of Holiness

"Let Us go down and there confuse their language, that they may not understand one another's speech" (11:7).

Then they were all amazed and marveled, saying to one another . . . "how *is it that* we hear . . . them speaking in our own tongues the wonderful works of God" (Acts 2:7, 8, 11).

In Genesis 11 we read that God caused confusion of tongues so that the people could no longer understand each other. In Acts 2, on the Day of Pentecost with the personal advent of the Holy Spirit, God enabled people of many languages to understand each other. The key lies in the purpose behind the understanding: the Holy Spirit works only to glorify Jesus Christ, and that was the purpose of the gathering, the unity, on the Day of Pentecost. What a contrast to the purpose of the gathering on the plain of Shinar! Here is the antithesis to the unity of sin: the unity of holiness.

The Holy Spirit delivers us from independent individuality and builds us into the mystical body of Christ. The baptism with the Holy Spirit is a personal experience that makes individual Christians one in the Lord. The gifts of the Spirit are not for individual self-exaltation, but for the good of the whole body and the glorification of the Head.

God is the architect of the body of Christ, which is composed of those who have experienced regeneration and sanctification, and this body is the habitation of the Holy Spirit (see Ephesians 2:19–22). The saints meet together as one through this ministry of the Holy Spirit, not through external organizations. The body of Christ is an organism, not an organization.

What a lesson for those among us burning with the foolish fever of our day—the fever of intense activity for God. Organizing this; reorganizing that. When what is wanted is the movement of the Holy Spirit so that we may be one, as He is One (see John 17:21). This is "the unity of the Spirit in the bond of peace" (see Ephesians 4:3).

There is no danger of confusion when the Holy Spirit, as the unifying agent, has His right of way in the body of Christ. Remember, when there was the danger of estimating gifts above grace in the church at Corinth, when there was a chaotic babel of confusion, the apostle Paul had to take the matter in hand with his glowing wisdom to bring about ordered shape and growth.

There seem always to be new views abroad that would form a federation of nations or denominations of one kind and another. But unity can only come about through the Lord Jesus Christ and our adherence to Him and His purposes. Whenever a religious community or movement begins to organize, it seems to lose its life. Those who were once keen on proclaiming the Gospel are now bent only on the success of the organization.

Thank God there is a time coming when this earth will be His habitation. At present it is usurped by the world systems of men; when these Babels disappear, God's new heaven and earth will emerge. We will see "the holy city, New Jerusalem, coming down out of heaven from God, prepared as a bride adorned for her husband. . . . and He will dwell with [us], and [we] shall be His people. God Himself will be with [us] *and be* [our] God" (Revelation 21:2, 3).

Genesis 12:1–3

Crossing the Bar

Now the LORD had said to Abram:

"Get out of your country,
From your family
And from your father's house,
To a land that I will show you" (12:1).

Alfred, Lord Tennyson's famous poem "Crossing the Bar" is a picture of what happens whenever we act in faith in God: "Sunset and evening star, \ And one clear call for me!"

Whatever the direction God indicates, we have to launch right out in faith. God's call always offers the possibility of refusal on our part, of course, for when He calls us, He does not tell us what to expect. He hands us sealed orders and urges us to a vast venture. Faith never knows where it is being led; it only knows and loves the One who is leading. We may not know where we are going, but we know who is making us go.

Each of us can find inspiration and explanation for the personal, private life of faith by examining the life of Abraham, often called the Father of the Faithful. Abraham's example, with both his limitations as well as his obedience, is full of minute instruction with regard to the life of faith.

The Call of God

The call of God is implicit, never explicit. It is like the call of the sea or the mountains: no one hears these calls but the one who has the nature of the sea or the mountains; and no one hears the call of God who has not the nature of God in him. The call of God is a call into comradeship with the Lord Himself for His own purposes, and the test of faith is to believe that God knows what He is about.

When God says "Follow Me," He never says to where; the itinerary must be left entirely to Him. We come in with our "but" and "supposing" and "what will happen if I do?" (see Luke 9:57–62). We have nothing to do with what will happen if we obey; we have to abandon to God's call in unconditional surrender, leaving behind all our shivering wisdom, and smilingly wash our hands of the consequences. However, this does not mean that a life of faith is a life of fate. Fate is stoical resignation to an unknown force. Faith is commitment to One whose character we know because it has been revealed to us in Jesus Christ. And as we live in contact with our heavenly Father, His order comes to us in the haphazard, and we recognize that every detail of our lives is engineered by Him.

The call of God only becomes clear as we obey, never as we weigh the pros and cons and try to reason it out. The call is God's idea, not our idea; and only on looking back over the path of obedience do we realize what God's idea has been all along, for God sanctifies memory. When we hear the call of God it is not for us to dispute with Him and arrange to obey Him if He will expound the meaning of His call to us. As long as we insist on having the call explained, we will never obey. But when we obey, it all becomes clear, so that looking back we can say with a chuckle of confidence, "He doeth all things well." Before us there is nothing, but overhead there is God, and we have to trust Him.

The Calling of Abraham

> By faith Abraham obeyed when he was called to go out to the place which he would receive as an inheritance. And he went out not knowing where he was going (Hebrews 11:8).

One of the hardest lessons to learn is the one which describes Abraham in the New Testament roll call of faith. "He went out not knowing where he was going" could be said of a faithful soul or a fool—or perhaps both. For as we, like Abraham, obey the call of God, we often become fools in the eyes of the world.

In the beginning faith is always uncertain, because at that point we have only the broad view, uncertain of particulars. We hear the call of God while we listen to a sermon or during a time of prayer, and we say, "Yes, I will give myself to God unreservedly." Then something happens in our immediate circumstances that does not seem to fit into the vision we have had, and the danger is that we might compromise and say we must have been mistaken in the vision. Our natural tendency is to want to be always on the mountain where the view is clear. When we come down into the Devil-possessed valley we get annoyed or exhausted, thinking we cannot go on with God there. We have perfect faith in God as long as He keeps us on the mount, but not the slightest atom of faith when He takes us into the valley. Yet it is the trial of our faith that lies in these particulars, and it is in passing through that trial that we become spiritually enriched.

> "Get out of your country, from your family and from your father's house" (12:1).

Personal acquaintance with God shows itself in separation, symbolized by Abraham's physical separation from his country and his kindred. Jesus Himself emphasized this need for separation (see Luke 14:26). Nowadays, such separation often involves a moral rather than a physical severance as we detach ourselves from the way those nearest and dearest to us think and look at things, if they do not have a personal relationship with God.

Those who would argue against obeying the call of God frequently take the shape of country and kindred, and if we listen to them, our ears will soon become dull to God's call. Their sympathy competes with God for the throne of our life, and we dissolve into the most commonplace Christians imaginable because we have no courage to strike out in faith. We have seen and heard but have not gone on. If we accept sympathy from those who have not heard the call of God, it will so blunt our own sense of His call that we become useless to Him.

Ultimately, every saint stands alone before God. And when He calls us to step out in faith, we begin the walk of faith alone, seeking no other comrade than the One who has called us for His purpose.

Genesis 12:4–9

On with God

So Abram departed (12:4).

It is not only sin and disobedience that keep us from obey-ing the call of God, but the good, right, natural things that make us hesitate. The natural can only be transformed into the spiritual by obedience, and the beginnings of God's life in a man or woman cut directly across the will of nature. The call of God comes with a realization that what He says is true, but that does not prevent us from agonizing over actual details of that call as we go through the trial of our faith. And it is when we deal with details that we begin to dispute with God and say, "But if I obey You here, what will happen there?" To respond in this way means we do not believe God one atom, although we say we do.

The knowledge of God's will is not like working out a mathematical problem ahead of time; only as we obey does His will for us become as clear as daylight. We have to be con-tinually renewed in the spirit of our minds, refusing to be conformed to the spirit of the age in which we live; only then do we "prove"—literally, work out in obedience—"what *is* that good and acceptable and perfect will of God" (see Romans 12:2). We must beware of giving credit to man's wisdom for the way he has taken, when all the time it is the perfect

wisdom of God that is manifested through the simple obedience of the man. It is never the acute ability of the saint that
is exhibited, but the astute wisdom of God.

The Concession of Abraham's Faith (12:4)

Faith in God always demands a concession from us personally. Abraham went on with God, as God had commanded,
although he did not really know where he was going. Watch
the debates that go on in our minds when God speaks: whether
it is in a big or small matter, we won't launch out on God's
command; we would rather hug the shoreline. If we are going
to obey God, there must be a concession made on our part; we
deliberately have to trust the character of God in the face of all
obstacles. "If God would only come down and explain everything to me, I would have faith in Him," we say. And yet how
little trust we really have in Him, even when we have experienced His grace and a revelation of Himself. We sink back to
the experience instead of being confident in the God who gave
us the experience.

Experience is never the ground of our trust; it is only the
gateway to the One in whom we trust. The work of faith is not
an explanation but a determination to obey God and to make a
concession of our faith in His character. As soon as we do
what God says, we discern what He means.

The natural man insists on explanations, because whatever
he can explain, he can command. In the spiritual domain nothing is explained until we obey, and then it is not so much an
explanation as an instant discernment. "If anyone wills to do
His will, he shall know . . ." (see John 7:17). If we say, "I want
to know why I should do this," it means we have no faith in
God, only sordid confidence in our own wits. We idolize our
own wisdom and ability and need to "understand." We do not
mind being saints if we can be saints on our own terms and

initiative. If we can instruct God about our upbringing and our particular temperament and affinities, if we can construct the scenery, then we would like to be saints.

It is the hesitation of the natural refusing to be transformed into the spiritual. In Abraham there was no such hesitation, although there were misinterpretations at times. Abraham made a confession of his faith to God, and "departed as the LORD had spoken to him."

The Companions of Abraham's Faith (12:5)

To live a life alone with God does not mean that we live it apart from everyone else. The connection between godly men and women and those folks associated with them is continually revealed in the Bible. If you are going on with God, says Paul, you will "labor and suffer reproach, because [you] trust in the living God" (1 Timothy 4:10). However, though your personal revelation may not be theirs, if you remain faithful to those immediate relationships, God will undertake to instruct them. Often it is as they see your witness as you "labor and suffer reproach" that those around you come to faith in the Lord.

The Consecration of Abraham's Faith (12:6–9)

Here we see that early in his journey of faith, Abraham built an altar in worship to God. Worship is the tryst of sacramental identification with God; that is, we deliberately give back to God the best He has given us, that we may be identified with Him in it. Later we see that whenever Abraham neglected to build an altar after God had made a promise to him, he fell into sin.

Worship is the most personally sacred act that God demands of His faithful ones. Whenever God has given us a blessing, we must take time to meditate on the blessing and offer it back to God in a deliberate ecstasy of worship. He never allows us to hug a spiritual blessing to ourselves; it has to be given back to Him so that He may make it a blessing to others. If we hoard our blessings, they will turn to spiritual dry rot. If God has blessed you, erect an altar and give the blessing back to God as a love-gift.

Abraham pitched his tent between Bethel and Ai. Bethel is the symbol of communion with God; Ai is the symbol of the world. The measure of the worth of our public activity for God is the private, profound communion we have with Him.

Some of us like to play spiritual leapfrog, jumping from worship to waiting and from waiting to work, as though somehow we must divide ourselves among these three states. God intends that the three should go together as they were in the disciplined life of our Lord. He was unhasting and unresting. There is plenty of time to worship God, if we will only take the time to pitch our tents and erect our altars.

Genesis 12:10–13

The Dance of Circumstances

Now there was a famine in the land (12:10).

There is a difference between circumstances and environment. We cannot control our circumstances, but we can
choose our environment. Environment is the element in our
circumstances which fits the individual disposition. A man
convicted of sin and a man in love may be in the same external
circumstances, but the environment of the one is totally different from that of the other. Our environment depends upon
our personal reaction to circumstances. Circumstances may
dance around us perplexingly, beyond our control, but that
does not mean that we cannot control ourselves in the midst of
those circumstances. It is in our reaction to those circumstances that we must exhibit a personal relationship to the
highest we know. Only by living in the presence of God do we
cease to act in an ungodlike manner in perplexing circumstances.

The Famine in the Land of Promise (12:10)

We hear God's call on the mount, but when the dance of
circumstances begins, we forget that we have to react to those

circumstances in accordance with our faith in God. This is what happened to Abraham. Surely the famine must have been a severe test of his faith; but in going down to Egypt, Abraham failed the test.

We must never lose sight of the necessity for discipline in the life of faith; only by means of this discipline are we taught the difference between the natural interpretation of what we call good and what God means by good. We have to be brought to the place of hearty agreement with God as to what He means by good, and we only reach it by the trial of our faith, never by a stoical effort that says, "Well, I must make up my mind that this is God's will, and that it is best."

At times it appears as if God has not only forsaken His word, but has deliberately deceived us. We asked Him for a particular thing, or related to Him in a certain way, and expected that it would mean the fullness of blessing. What we got was just the opposite—upset, trouble, and difficulty all around—and we are staggered, until we learn that by this very discipline God is bringing us to the place of entire abandonment to Himself.

Never settle down in the middle of the dance of circumstances and say that you have been mistaken in your natural interpretation of God's promise to you because the immediate aftermath is devastation. Say that God did give the promise, and stick to it, and slowly God will bring you into the perfect, detailed fulfillment of that promise. When and where the fulfillment will take place depends upon God; but never doubt the absolute fulfillment of God's word, and remember that the beginning of the fulfillment lies in your acquiescence to His will.

Remain true to God, even though it means that His sword

must pierce through your natural inclinations, bringing you into a supernaturally clear agreement with Him. We are not introduced to Christianity by explanations, but we must labor at the exposition of Christianity until we satisfactorily unfold it through God's grace and our own effort.

The Foreboding on the Line of Peace (12:11–13)

Whenever expediency comes in, that cunning rascal brings in its train a foreboding anxiety, which is a sure sign that in that particular we are ceasing to obey God. Our personal testimony must attest unmistakably to the whole of the truth, not to part of it. Whenever we are hesitant to give public witness to that which God has revealed, when we begin to get dexterous in juggling what truth we will tell, it is a dexterity that is more or less doubtful. We speak the truth, but not the whole truth. In our doubtful weighing of things we are not relying on God, but are placing presumptuous confidence and trust in our own wits. God will see us though only if we stand steadfastly true to what He has told us.

Another danger is to imagine that it is our particular presentation of things that will attract people. It may well attract them, but never to God. If we attract others by personal impressiveness, the attracted will get no further than us. Our Lord said, "And I, if I am lifted up . . . will draw all *peoples* to Myself" (John 12:32).

This verse reveals a weakness in Abraham's faith. He does not yet perfectly rely upon the help of God in God's own way and time. This weakness arises from his inability to apply his faith in God to the actual circumstances he is in. We have to be true to God, not to our idea of God.

If we imagine we have any strength apart from God, we

will have to break the neck of our strength over some obstacle before we are willing to rely upon Him. Our own strength is the backbone of the natural life, but not the life of God. There will be a wobble in our walk of faith until the vision of faith and the reality are one and the same.

Genesis 12:14–20

Blank Astonishment

What *is* this you have done to me? (12:18).

When we sin directly, we are never blankly astonished at the result. We may be defiant; we may be untruthful; or we may even accept God's forgiveness. Blank astonishment comes when we fail to do God's will in spite of our very desire to do it—as did Abraham. We see no word of censure here for Abraham's distinct failure in going down to Egypt to escape the famine in the land God had promised him, but the blank astonishment which it caused is implied.

At this point we must beware of saying what Abraham ought to have done: first, because he did not do it; and second, because in doing so we increase the severity of our own condemnation. This incident is not related to dishonor Abraham, but to honor God.

Note that Abraham did not attempt to vindicate himself, nor should we. We must beware of thinking—no matter what we say—that God guided us in our wrong decisions. This leads to spiritual hypocrisy. God holds His children responsible for the way in which they interpret His will. We only discern God's will by being renewed in the spirit of our minds in every circumstance. We must learn to tell ourselves the truth on the basis of God's word, not on the basis of independent spiritual impulse.

The Saint's Guilt in the Worldling's Sin
(12:14–16)

The result of Abraham's going down to Egypt was perplexity for himself and responsibility for giving Pharaoh a direct occasion to sin. Despite this, Pharaoh treats Abraham with a generosity which must have put Abraham to shame.

At times an eager desire to serve God can lead us to transgress God's order, affecting not only our own lives, but the lives of those around us. Our own poor judgment can present others with an occasion for sin. Then the eager saint says in blank astonishment, "But I only wanted to do God's will."

In his eagerness to do the right thing, Abraham transgressed, but his act was not a moral sin. Transgression is nearly always an unconscious act rather than a conscious determination to do wrong. Sin is never an unconscious act. We must be careful to discern between the two.

The striking thing in our Lord's life was that He was not more eager to do the will of His Father than His Father was for Him to do it. He was the Savior of the world, everything depended upon Him, and yet for thirty years He lived an ordinary, obscure life. "His doing nothing wonderful was in itself a kind of wonder," said Saint Bonaventure. Our Lord's life was the exhibition of *the will of God,* not of *doing* the will of God.

The Saint's Gifts from the Worldling's Sincerity
(12:16)

The Egyptian maid Hagar who became so important an influence in the lives of Abraham and Sarah was probably one of the gifts given to Abraham in Egypt. While the friendships and gifts of the world may be perfectly sincere, the saint soon realizes that these can be embarrassing and hindering if he is to remain loyal to God. Then begins the blank astonishment of real perplexity, and God never shields us from anxiety on this score. It is not a case of right and wrong, but of learning through chastening what Abraham learned: that we cannot come eagerly and find out God's will by guessing. We must be renewed in our minds in every circumstance and beware of suspicions and considerations and suggestions that make themselves seem right to us. We must beware of despising the chastening of the Lord or of fainting when we are rebuked by Him. The only thing to do is to be silent about our blank astonishment and go on to the next thing.

The Saint's Groaning and the Worldling's Scorn (12:17–18)

Pharaoh seems to have been a wise man, for he concludes that the judgment on his house is from God because of Sarah. He reproaches Abraham scornfully for lying to him. Actually, Abraham did not tell a lie; in his fear, he told a half-truth (see Genesis 20:12).

To say that if a man commits sin he will hinder the purpose of God is not true; however, if a *leader* tries to serve his own ends, he will hinder the purpose of God. For instance, if I were to try to use the house of God for my own ends, the atmosphere of the house would be damaged instantly. Personal sin does not present a barrier in God's house, although it does put a barrier between the one who is sinning and God. But as soon as anyone tries to use God's house, or God's people, or God's things for his own purposes and ends, then the atmosphere is altered at once. When this occurs, it produces the groaning of the saint and the scorn of the worldling, and the humiliating thing is that in such a case the worldling is right.

The Saint's Grade in the Worldling's Separation
(12:19–20)

Abraham was dismissed by Pharaoh—a most unspeakable humiliation. If in our eagerness to stand for God's honor we have compromised, we will have to endure, as Abraham did, the scorn of the honorable worldling. Instead of *our* breaking from the world, the world will break with us. Then, by our very desire to stand up loyally for God, we have put ourselves in a position where we cannot stand up for Him. The discipline of our lives is to become as little children. A little child would have stayed in the land whether there was a famine or not.

Abraham's trip to Egypt and his transgressions there led to all the complexity that came afterward and account for the continual recurrence of Egypt in the history of the kingdom of God, until at last Egypt is to be united into the great, full purpose of God.

Genesis 13

Unperplexed

And [Abram] went on his journey from the South as far as
Bethel, to the place where his tent had been at the beginning
(13:3).

When we study the lives of the saints, we discover to our
confusion that from one standpoint they are a jumble of inconsistencies, while from another they are an exhibition of the
boundless consistency of God. The problem is our perspective.
If we study the life of a saint in order to find out what God is
like, we will finish up by throwing our hands in the air in
frustration. But if we study God Himself, we will find that He
manifests His amazing consistency in the weakest and feeblest
saint.

At one time we find Abraham in a blank and sordid muddle; at another he is unperplexed and noble. The point is that
God remains the same whether Abraham is unperplexed or
muddled.

The Tryst of Sacramental Identification (13:1–4)

The Way. Abraham went with God, and Lot went with
Abraham. Lot continually went to pieces; Abraham never did.
One lived a life of faithfulness, the other a life of faith. A life of
faithfulness is devotion to a servant of God; a life of *faith* is
devotion to God Himself.

The Wealth. Abraham and Lot came back from Egypt exceedingly wealthy, and the abundance of their possessions nearly brought about strife between them. But Abraham would not let his possessions keep him from his tryst with God. It is perilously possible to make your spiritual life depend on the abundance of things you possess, material or otherwise. When we are learning to trust God, He gives us at first certain things on which to lean; then if He withdraws them, we say it is the Devil. No, it is the chastening of the Lord because He sees that we are not only possessing those things; they are possessing us. If we are drawing our life from money, then God may well withdraw our money. We can only possess our possessions by being detached from them and attached to God who is the source of all. We have only one source, and that is God.

The Worship. All commentators notice one interesting fact about Abraham's life, and that is that whenever he neglected to erect an altar, he went astray. This is of great significance because worship is the tryst of sacramental identification. In worship we deliberately give back to God the best He has given us so that we may be identified with Him in it.

If Abraham had erected an altar, he would not have gone down to Egypt, but would have identified himself with God over the famine in the Land of Promise. Selfishness in spiritual matters rapidly produces delusion. If we go back to the place where we first built an altar to God, we will be delivered from the delusion of obtuse independent certainty. Worship is the sacramental element in the saint's life.

The Test of Self-Interest (13:5–13)

As surely as we begin our life of faith with God, fascinating, luxurious, and rich prospects will open to us, which are ours by right. But if we are living the life of faith, we will waive our rights and give them away, letting God choose for us. This is the discipline of transforming the natural into the spiritual by obedience to God's voice. In the life of faith God allows us to get into a place of testing where the consideration of our own welfare would be the right and proper thing if we were not living the life of faith; but if we are living the life of faith, we will heartily waive our own rights and let God choose for us. Whenever we make "our right" our guidance, we blunt our spiritual insight.

The greatest enemy of the life with God is not sin, but the good that is not good enough. It would have seemed the wisest thing in the world for Abraham to choose the land he wanted; it was his right, and the people round him would have considered him a fool for not choosing. Many of us do not go on in our spiritual life because we prefer to choose what is our right instead of relying upon God to choose for us. We have to learn to keep our eye on God as we walk.

The Tax of Riches. Abraham's riches were in a great measure a tax to him. Every possession is tainted with a want; and in this case the want was for sufficient pasturage. When Jesus Christ came He possessed nothing; the only symbol for our Lord is the symbol of poverty (see 2 Corinthians 8:9; Luke 9:58) and this should be true of the saint—"having nothing, and yet possessing all things." Every possession produces an appetite that clings.

The Touch of Rectitude. Lot forgot the place of communion; he thought only of the world. But Abraham, unperplexed, instantly exhibited forbearance as the result of his tryst with God. Abraham's rectitude was not the rectitude of honor, but of holiness. This rectitude is exhibited in the life of the holiest being who ever trod the earth, in the life of Jesus Christ, of whom it is recorded: "He pleased not Himself."

The Tarnish of Reasonableness. Lot chose to possess what he considered the best. This reasonableness, this selfish subjectivity, is what tarnishes a mind that has neglected its tryst with God.

The Type of Supreme Integrity (13:14–18)

The Manifestation of God. When God revealed Himself to Abraham, Abraham's faith was elevated. When God concealed Himself, Abraham's faith sank. The first manifestation of God to Abraham was in his migration to Canaan; the first concealing was when he went down to Egypt. Abraham did not have another manifestation of God until after his noble act of faith toward Lot.

The Message of God. Throughout Abraham's life there is a connection between the providence of God and Abraham's conduct. The promises of God correspond to the acts and conduct of faith in Abraham. Only when Abraham acts in accordance with his real faith in God, does God speak to him.

The Man of God. Paul takes Abraham as a type of the life of faith; not as the type of a saint, but of a tried faith built on a real God. The sanctification of our faith, as distinct from the sanctification of our heart, is the unfathomable, supernatural blessing from God.

Genesis 14:1–16

War

Now when Abram heard that his brother was taken captive, he armed his three hundred and eighteen trained *servants* who were born in his own house, and went in pursuit as far as Dan (14:14).

In the study of Abraham, as in the study of all Bible characters, principles are no guide. The inconsistencies we find in Abraham reveal the consistency of God, and the thing to note is that Abraham remained true to God both before and after his lapses. The basis of truth is not an abstraction or a principle, but a personal relationship. Reality is not found in logic; Reality is a Person. "I am the Truth," Jesus said. Spiritual life is based on a personal relationship to Jesus Christ and on the consequent responsibility of that relationship.

The Way of Violence (14:1–8)

This is the first war mentioned in Scripture, and its cause was the lust for dominion. The way of the world against the world is portrayed in this chapter, and it is full of the most intense spiritual interpretation. Life without conflict is impossible, either in nature or in grace. This is a fact of life. The basis of physical, mental, moral, and spiritual life is antagonism.

Physical life is maintained by the power of fight in the corpuscles of the blood. If we have sufficient vital force within to overcome the forces without, we produce the balance of health. The same is true of the mind. If we want to maintain a clear, vigorous mental life, we have to fight to produce the balance of thought. Morally it is the same. If we have sufficient moral fighting capacity, we produce the moral balance of virtue. And spiritually it is the same. Everything that is not spiritual makes for our undoing. But Jesus tells us to be of "good cheer," for He has overcome the world. Once we understand this, it is a perfect delight to meet opposition, and as we learn to score off the things that come against us, we produce the balance of holiness. Faith must be tried, and it is the trial of faith that is precious.

The War of Fainthearted Defense (14:9–12)

When God's providence involves us unexpectedly in all sorts of complications, the test comes on two lines: Will I have faith in God? and Will I ally myself with those who rescue the downtrodden irrespective of their beliefs? It is instructive to note that in the Bible faintheartedness arises whenever self-interest begins to get luxurious. The sign of faintheartedness in individuals is in the languid talk of "someone else" when there is anything to be done.

Whenever you begin to experience fatigue or weariness or degradation, you may be certain you have done one of two things: either you have disregarded a law of nature or you have deliberately got out of touch with God. Once the warning note of weariness is sounded, it is a sign that something has gone wrong. That warning is God's wonderfully gentle way of saying, "Not that way; that must be left alone; this must be given up." Spiritual fatigue comes from the unconscious frittering away of God's time. When you feel weary or are exhausted, don't ask for hot milk; get back to God. The secret of weariness and nervous disease in the natural world is the lack of a dominant interest, and the same is true in spiritual life. Much of what is called Christian work is really veneered spiritual disease.

There is no such thing as weariness in God's work. If you are in tune with the joy of the Lord, the more you spend out in God's service, the more the recuperation goes on. When you are dominated by life from God, every moment is filled with an energy that is not your own, a super-abounding life that nothing can withstand.

The War of Divine Inspiration (14:13–16)

In chapter 13 Abraham was put through the test of self-interest, and here he is put through the test of self-complacency. It would have been so easy for Abraham to slip into the complacency of believing that what befell Lot was just and that God was proving Abraham to be right. But the patriarch did not fail the test; he did not sit down with a sanctified smirk and say, "Perhaps Lot will learn wisdom now." Instead, Abraham entered into the war with the light and cheerful heroism of heaven.

Whenever a conflict like the one pictured here takes place, the successful fighters are the faithful children of the faithful saints: "*servants* who were born in his own house." In the natural world there are three—father, mother, and child; and in the spiritual world there are three—God, church, and converts. If a spiritual nature cannot reproduce its own kind, it will have to answer to God for it. In spiritual warfare, may God have mercy on the barren saint who has never produced his own kind but has to rely upon the converts of others.

Genesis 14:17–24

More Than Conqueror

"Blessed be Abram of God Most High, possessor of heaven and earth; and blessed be God Most High, who has delivered your enemies into your hand" (14:19–20).

We have to live perfectly actual lives, not actually perfect lives. This fact makes all the difference between religious faith and religious farce, and is very clearly brought out in the life of Abraham. God is not actual, He is real, and He bears into me His Holy Spirit who enables me to live a perfectly actual life, kept by the reality of the love of God.

"I don't feel this and that," we say. How can we, when God is not actual, but real? Feeling has to do with actualities and will come later. Right feeling is produced by obedience, never the reverse. We are brought into contact with actuality by our senses, and into contact with reality by our faith. The test in actual things is: Am I living a life of faith, or a life of common sense which denies faith? Faith does not make me *actually perfect*; faith makes me *perfectly actual*.

When the Victory Is Won (14:17)

The supreme test in the perfectly actual life of faith comes after a victory has been gained. In the expansive hour of relaxation the ruling disposition of the heart is instantly manifested.

67

We read that after a day when "the whole city was gathered together at the door," our Lord rose up a great while before day in order to pray, not to praise (see Mark 1:32–35). In Abraham, the victory revealed that he was more than conqueror over himself. To say "I have got the victory" is a selfish testimony; the testimony of the Spirit of God is that "the Victor has got me." If we can claim victories for ourselves, we are not in right relationship to God at that particular time. Instead of worshiping God, we are conscious only of what He has done through us, and we triumph in the experience He has brought us. My actual life is given me by God, and I can live in it either as an atheist or as a worshiper. Abraham was a man who worshiped God after a victory.

Where the Victor Is a Worshiper (14:18–20)

Abraham was a man who worshiped God after a victory. Yet just when Abraham stands as the most striking character, Melchizedek enters and towers above him.

> What better type or symbol could there be of the absolute, the everlasting, the divine high priesthood and kingship than that phenomenal figure of Melchizedek? He comes out of the invisible, timeless eternity of the past; he belongs to the timeless assured eternity of the future; he is High Priest forever. (DuBose)

Melchizedek is a type of Christ, whereas Abraham is a type of the perfectly actual children of God. Melchizedek represents the incarnation of God; Abraham represents the life of faith in the God who became incarnate. "Christ in me" and "I in Christ"; "Christ the Lord" and "Christ the Servant"—all become simple when we understand the relationship of Melchizedek and Abraham.

The supreme lesson of the perfectly actual life of faith is to learn how to worship. Faith brings us into personal contact with God before whom we must ever bow. We have to maintain a worshipful relationship to God in everything, and in the beginning this is difficult. We are all right at meetings, at anything that is illuminated, but when it comes to actual life, we are actually of no use. We can talk till we receive further orders, but don't ask us to live the life.

We have to contend for God in our actual circumstances, and our contention for God lies in seeing that we rely upon Him absolutely while we carry out the dictates of our faith in Him. Melchizedek brings bread and wine to refresh the heroes of the perfectly actual life. Christ never takes part in the perfectly actual mix-up of our human lives; therefore, to ask, "What would Jesus do?" is not the question of faith but of Pharisaism. The question to ask is, "What would Jesus have *me* do?" It is impossible for Christ to be where we are; that is why He has put us there. We have to put on the new man in the actual circumstances we are in and manifest Him. It is arrogant humbug to imagine we are to be God Almighty on this earth. We are to be the sons and daughters of God, to live actual lives and put on the new man by deliberate acts of faith all the time, not denying the actual life. We have to remember that our bodies are the temples of the Holy Ghost and to see that God is manifested in our mortal flesh by our worship; and that can only be done as we take the nourishment, the bread and the wine, that will sustain us in our actual contentions for God.

It is dangerous to take Abraham as the picture of sanctification. Sanctification means the perfection of Jesus Christ manifesting itself in actual experience. If we take Abraham as a picture of sanctification, we will have to chop his life up and say, This part is sanctification, and that is not. And in doing so, we will produce a false spiritual interpretation. Abraham is a picture of the life of faith, not the result of faith. He portrays for all time the ups and downs, the haphazards and the tests, the nobilities and the blunders of the perfectly actual life of faith.

While the Victorious Is Worthy (14:21–24)

Abraham renounced any advantage for himself, but he preserved the rights of those with him. We have the perfect right not to insist on our rights, for it is the privilege of a Christian to waive his rights; but we do not always recognize that we must insist on those associated with us getting their rights. If they prefer to take the line of faith that we take, that is their responsibility. But we are not exonerated from seeing that they get their rights.

A Star-Hitched Wagon

And he believed in the Lord (15:6).

There is a wildness in God's expectations. If only He had told us to hitch our wagon to a mule, we could see how it might be done; but to tell us to hitch our natural lumbering wagons to the star of Almighty God makes us wonder whether we have understood Him aright. Faith sticks to the wagon and the star; fanaticism jumps from the wagon to the star and breaks its neck. A saint is not an angel and never will be; a saint is flesh and blood and lives in the theater in which the decrees of God are carried to successful issues. All of which means that God demands of us the doing of common things while we abide in Him.

The Vision in the Valley of Afterward (15:1)

The meaning of the valley of afterward is that there must be an interchange between actualities and realities, for it is the successful interchange between the two that keeps the life healthy. There is no afterward to the one who lives his life mystically only; a life that produces no results is an intensely selfish life. There must be the interchange between our real standing before God and our life on the earth. Our wagon must be hitched to the star, and hitched to it by faith.

71

The afterward of success for God produces the feeling: Was it worthwhile? The coward fears before danger; the heroic spirit fears afterward. It was after the victory, when Abraham went into the Valley of Afterward that God said to him, "Do not be afraid. . . ."

If you say, "My goal is God Himself" before you have been to school, it is merely a nursery rhyme. But say it after winning a victory that tells for God, and the victory does not seem such a glorious thing after all—until you find that the goal is not a prize, but the fulfillment of a decree of God in and through you.

The Veil on the Vision of Abraham (15:2–3)

Abraham was not rebellious, but he also was not hilarious. He believed that Eliezer must be his heir, and he acquiesced in the purpose of God. He only wanted light as to the meaning of it. His exclamation, "Look, You have given me no offspring," was not a murmur against God, but a pious exclamation of weakness. It was not a challenge to God, but an expression of resignation. Abraham was blaming himself for misinterpreting God: "Excuse me for being so disappointed, Lord, but I find that all my hopes and ideas have been wrong."

Abraham is not pitying himself, but pitying God's reputation in himself; he cannot understand how God is going to fulfill what He has promised. He has no heir other than Eliezer; therefore, the idea of having a child must have been a misinterpretation. The veil on the vision of Abraham makes him say: "It can't be done; I want an explanation as to Your meaning."

If any promise of God is not being fulfilled, beware of saying, "Oh, well, I must have misinterpreted what God meant." We have to build in absolute confidence on God. There is nothing more heroic than to have faith in God when you can see so many better things in which to have faith. It is one thing to have faith before the fact—when in the midst of despair you will hope for anything. It is quite another to have faith in God after a tremendous victory has been won, and then in the aftermath to see no clear realization of that for which God had caused you to hope.

The Voice and the Vastness of Altitude (15:4–5)

In this chapter we fathom the depths of all that the New Testament unfolds. Abraham the childless is to become the father of nations. How mad the promise sounds! God points Abraham away from his wagon in the mud to that starry night and hitches the two together by His own word. God's appeal to the stars is not to furnish proof for a doubting mind, but to provide nourishment for a faltering faith. Nature to the saint is a sacrament of God, not merely a series of facts; not symbols and signs, but the real evidence of the coming of God as a sacrament to His faithful children.

The whole discipline of the life of faith is to mix together the light of heaven and the sordid actuality of earth. Contemplation and consideration must go together. We must take our plan for what we do on earth from the altitude of heaven; let contemplation of the stars be mixed with what we build on earth.

Living in the dumps and living in a hurry are worse than the Devil and are both excessively culpable. Living in the dumps is an absolute slur against God: I won't look up. I have done all I could but it is all over, and I am in despair. Hurry is the same mood expressed in an opposite way: I have no time to pray, no time to look to God or to consider anything; I must do the thing. Perspiration is mistaken for inspiration, and we drive our miserable little wagon in a rut instead of hitching it to a star and pulling according to God's plan.

God hitched Abraham's wagon to the stars He had created, by His word. In our personal lives the great solution is always found in the words of our Lord when we have His Spirit. Jesus Christ is God incarnate, and He makes His words spirit and life to us. Our little human wagons are hitched to the star of God's sacramental purpose by the words of Jesus and in no other way. Whenever we indulge in hurry or in the dumps and refuse to pay attention to His words, we smash the connecting line and go off on our own.

The Veracity and Virtue of Attitude (15:6)

"And he believed in the LORD, and He accounted it to him for righteousness." This is the act by which Abraham goes out of himself and relies upon God for righteousness and grace. Abraham had manifested many noble qualities of heart and many virtues in his walk of faith, but these did not make him righteous before God. That was accomplished through his living confidence in God.

This verse is the first germ of the great doctrine of "the Lord our Righteousness." Righteousness must never be made to mean less than a guiltless position in the presence of justice and right. The justification of every sinner is by faith, and by faith alone. But it is our just walk that proves Him just in saving us. If we do not walk in the life of faith, we are a slander to God.

Genesis 16:1–6

Good Versus Best

> Then Sarai, Abram's wife, took Hagar her maid, the Egyptian, and gave her to her husband Abram to be his wife (16:3).

In the spiritual life we do not go from good to better, and from better to best; there is only One to whom we go, and that One is The Best, God Himself. There can be no such thing as God's second best. We can perversely put ourselves out of God's order into His permissive will, but that is a different matter. In seeking the best we soon find that the things that keep us from God's best are not sin and imperfection, but the things that are right and good and noble from the natural standpoint. To discern that the natural virtues antagonize surrender to God is to bring our soul at once into the center of our greatest battlefield. Very few of us debate with the sordid and the wrong, but we do debate with the good; and the higher up we go in the scale of the natural virtues, the more intense is the opposition to Jesus Christ.

The Fanaticism of Self-denial (16:1–2)

The childless state of Abraham's house was its great sorrow, and was a constant trial to Abraham's faith. Abraham's call was dependent upon his having seed. Abraham and Sarah did their best to fulfill God's command, but in so doing they got out of God's order into His permissive will. The fanatic, passionate desire to fulfill God's will led them into desperate error.

There is a lesson here for us, too: beware of the fanaticism of self-denial, for it will lead to error with lasting effects. When we go off on that line we become devoted to our interpretation of our destiny. Destiny is never abstract. The destiny of a human being is vested in personal relationship to God. Abraham learned this lesson later; on Mount Moriah he proved that he knew the difference between obeying what God said and obeying the God who said it. Fanaticism is sticking true to my interpretation of my destiny instead of waiting for God to make it clear. The fanatic's line is: *Do* something. The test of faith lies in not doing.

Natural impulse in a saint leads to perdition unless it is brought into obedience to the destiny of God and turned into inspiration. It is not that impulse is wrong, but it will lead to wrong unless it is brought into obedience to the spiritual destiny of the life, and this can only be done by devotion to the One who founds our destiny for us, our Lord Himself. Beware of trying to forestall God's program by your own impulse.

The Falsity of Sagacious Discernment (16:3–4)

Abraham and Sarah both adhered to their sagacious discernment in acting in accordance with the practice of the time in which they lived. In acting according to their own acute discernment, however, they began dictating to God about how His word must be fulfilled. They were leaning on their own understanding instead of trusting in the Lord with all their hearts.

Never say, God must do this thing. He must not; faith will fulfill His own word. We have no business dictating to Him.

We only have to remain true to God, and when His word is fulfilled we will know it because it will be a supernatural fulfillment. Always beware of being more eager to do God's will than God is for you to do it.

The remarkable thing about the life of our Lord was not that He was eager to do God's will, but that He was *obedient* to do it. He never put His fingers across the threads of His Father's providential order and gave a tug saying, "Now I will help You," thus pulling the thing right out of His Father's hands. He simply obeyed, leaving His Father's wisdom to arrange all for Him. Like Sarah and Abraham, we rush in and say, "I see what God wants and I will do it," and we wound our own souls and injure other lives.

The Fanaticism of Sensual Dominion (16:5–6)

Sarah's passionate outbreak and her subsequent harsh treatment of her maid Hagar are examples of the way we wound our own souls and injure other lives when we try to take God's providence into our own hands. Through her harsh treatment of Hagar, Sarah evidently thrust her back into the position of a mere slave; and Hagar, who believed she had risen above that position, fled. Hagar does not stand for sin, for Hagar and her son received real protection and blessing from God.

Hagar represents the natural life when it gets out of place and takes precedence over the spiritual life. Our natural life must be in subordination and under the absolute control of the spiritual. The natural must be turned into the spiritual by obedience, whatever sword has to go through its heart. The characteristic of the natural life is the independent passion for free dominion over itself. Thus, it is not only sin that produces the havoc in life; it is also the good opposing the best—the natural inclination and determination to "boss the show" for God and everyone else.

Genesis 16:7–16

Continuous Conversion

> Then [Hagar] called the name of the LORD who spoke to
> her, You-Are-the-God-Who-Sees (16:13).

Hagar represents the natural life; she does not represent
sin. Sin cannot be converted, and Hagar was. She is, however,
an excellent example of how we must continually convert the
natural life into submission to the Spirit of God in us. We can
never say, "I will never do anything natural again." That is the
delusion of fanaticism. When by the providence of God our
body is brought into new conditions, we have to see that our
natural life is converted to the dictates of the Spirit of God in
us. Because it has been done once is no proof that it will be
done again.

The attitude of continuous conversion is the only right
attitude toward the natural life. All the days of the saintly life
we must continually turn to God. Yet this is the one thing we
object to. Either we say the natural is wrong and try to kill it,
or else we say that the natural is all there is and that everything natural and impulsive is right. Neither attitude is right.
The hindrance in spiritual life is that we will not be continu-
ously converted, but in obstinate pride will spit at the throne
of God and say, "I am going to be boss." We cannot remain
boss by the sheer power of will, however; sooner or later our

wills must yield allegiance to some force greater than their own—either God or the Devil.

The Angel of the Lord and Wrecked Passion (16:7)

In her helpless condition, Hagar was in a fit state for the angel of the Lord to appear to her. Sarah's fanatic self-denial and vindictive spite were far from right, but they did not justify Hagar's passionate response. She alone was responsible for the wrong she did. Hagar desired to be the mother of the seed of Abraham. In her own mind she insisted on being not only equal with Sarah, but on displacing her in Abraham's affection and in God's plan.

Passion is the combination of desire and pride with a wild reach of possibility. The desire may be for a big thing or a little thing, but the instant result lands us in a wilderness of disgust, nursing wounded pride. Passion makes us reach for position, and it ends in spiritual infamy.

The right relationship of Hagar to Sarah represents the relationship of the natural life to the domination of the Holy Ghost. The natural life must not rule; the spiritual must rule, and it must rule over the natural life. We have to convert the natural life continually into submission to the Spirit of God in us.

The Angel of the Lord and Wounded Pride (16:8–9)

The angel of the Lord and conscience say the same thing—*return* and *submit*—yet they stand distinct. If the voice of God does not correspond with the voice of conscience, we need pay no heed to the latter. But when the voice of God says the same thing as conscience, we must either obey or be damned in that particular. Return from assumed responsibility and submit—to the old oppression? Yes, but without the elements of passion and pride, and the result will be according to the will of God.

Natural pride has to do with our standing before men—I shall not bow; I will make others bow to me. That is natural domination, and represents the antagonism of the natural life to the domination of the Holy Spirit. Wherever there is natural pride the Lord must inevitably be put to open shame.

The Angel of the Lord and the Word of Promise (16:10–12)

Throughout the Bible this is the revelation of the personal attitude of God to the miseries of the world: "I have heard your affliction." He is not indifferent; the cry does not go up to the ears of a deaf God.

Hagar's great desire was to be the mother of the believing children of Abraham, but the Lord says, "No, Hagar is to be the mother of Ishmael, and Ishmael is to be blessed." The limitation of the promise is connected with the promise itself. Hagar had to be cured of the delusion that she was destined to become the mother of the believing seed of Abraham. When God allowed Hagar and her son Ishmael to be cast out, they were being cast out of positions they had no right to hold (see 21:10 and Galatians 4:30).

The attitude of our Lord toward anything to do with the natural is unflinching, patient sternness; He is not cruel, but He is stern, just as He was stern with His mother (see John 2:4) and just as the apostle Paul was stern with his own body (see 1 Corinthians 9:27).

When we are born again, we enthrone Ishmael; that is, we consecrate our natural gifts and say, "These are the things with which God is going to do His work, and I have to see that they are put in the position of servants. If I put them on the throne, I start a mutiny within my own soul." The bondwoman and her child have to be cast out; the natural has to be sacrificed in order that it may be brought into perfect at-home-ness with the Spirit of God. If we make our natural life submit and obey the Holy Spirit within us, we hasten the time for the manifestation of the sons of God (see Romans 8:21).

The man who can rule his natural pride and virtue is able to take the city. Only when they have learned to bring the natural life into perfect submission to His ruling personality does God dare turn His saints loose.

The Appearing of the Lord and Waiting Patience (16:13–16)

"Then she called the name of the LORD . . . You-Are-the-God-Who-Sees" (16:13). Like Hagar, we never really see things as they are until we see God. When we see Him, we *see* for the first time. It is not the external things that look different; it is a different disposition that looks through the same eyes as the result of the internal surgery that has taken place. We see God, and then we see things as we have never seen them before.

Genesis 17:1

The Reservations of God

When Abram was ninety-nine years old, the LORD appeared to Abram and said to him, "I *am* Almighty God; walk before Me and be blameless" (17:1).

God is a perplexing being to man because He is never in the wrong, and through the process of allowing every bit of man's wrongdoing to appear right at the time, He proves Himself right ultimately. God never has to use His wits to keep Himself from being outwitted by man and the Devil. Individually we may thwart God's purpose in our lives for a time, but ultimately God's purpose will be fulfilled, wherever we end.

Human free will is God's sovereign work. We have power not to do God's will, and we have that power by the sovereign will of God; but we can never thwart God's will. God allows ample room for man and the Devil to do their worst. He allows the combination of other wills to work out to the last lap of exhaustion so that that way need never be tried again, and men will have to confess, reluctantly or willingly, that God's purpose was right after all. And this holds true in the individual lives of God's children. We are at liberty to try every independent plan of our own, but we shall find in the end—whether too late or not is another matter—that what God said we had better do at the beginning was the right thing, if only we had listened to Him.

In the life of Abraham, we see clearly the consequences of doing wrong, for every blunder Abraham made was repeated by his descendants. But the abiding truth remains, whether for Abraham or for us: this is not the result of cause and effect, but because God is God.

The Rigor of the Everlasting No

The word of the Lord came to Abraham in a vision. God's method always seems to be vision first and then reality, but in between the vision and the reality there is often a deep valley of humiliation ("and behold, horror *and* great darkness fell upon him" 15:12). How often has a faithful soul been plunged into a like darkness when after the vision has come the test. Whenever God gives a vision to a saint, He puts the saint in the shadow of His hand, as it were, and the saint's duty is to be still and listen. In chapters 15 and 16 we see the danger of listening to "good advice" in the dark instead of waiting for God to send the light.

When God gives a vision and darkness follows, wait; God will bring you into accordance with the vision He has given if you will await His timing. Otherwise, you try to do away with the supernatural in God's undertakings. Never try to help God fulfill His word. There are some things we cannot do, and that is one of them.

We must never try to anticipate the actual fulfillment of a vision. Often we transact some business spiritually with God on our mount of transfiguration and by faith see clearly a vision of His purpose; then immediately afterward there is nothing but blank darkness. We trust in the Lord, but we walk in darkness. At that point we are tempted to work up enthusiasm; instead, we are to wait on God. If darkness turns to spiritual doldrums, we are to blame. When God puts the dark of "nothing" into our experience, it is the most positive something He can give us. If we do anything at that point it is sure to be wrong. We have to remain in the center of nothing and say "Thank You" for it. When God gives us nothing it is because we are inside Him, and by determining to do something we put ourselves outside Him. This is a great lesson that few of us seem to learn.

Abraham would not stay in the land when the famine came because there was nothing; he would not trust God for a child because there was no one. God kept giving Abraham "nothing" (except Himself), and by determining to do "something" Abraham jumped outside God and found that he was putting himself in the relationship of the Everlasting No. There are things God tells us to do without any light or illumination other than the word of His command. All God's commands are enablings. We must not be weak in His strength.

Thirteen years have rolled by in between chapters 16 and 17, for Abraham had anticipated the purpose of God and had to pass through a long time of discipline. The act of Abraham and Sarah produced a complexity in God's plan that echoed down through the ages. In the same way, Moses had to wait forty years after his presumptuous attempt to reach his destination. Adam and Eve did the same thing when they tried to take the "shortcut" (which is the meaning of temptation) and anticipated their destination to be *actually* what they were *potentially* and thereby went wrong. Temptation does not spring from selfish lust, but from a passionate desire to reach God's destination.

Abraham emerged out of this stage of discipline with one determination: to let God have His way. There is no indication that he is relying on the flesh any longer; his reliance is on God alone. All self-sufficiency has been destroyed; there is not one common-sense ray left as to how God is going to fulfill His word. God never hastens and He never tarries. He works His plans out in His own way, and we either lie like clogs on His hands or we assist Him by being as clay in the hands of the potter.

Now Abraham sees the real God, not a vision. Such knowledge of the real God is reached when our confidence is placed in God and not in His blessings. Abraham's faith has become a tried faith built on a real God.

The Reality of the Everlasting Yea

God Almighty—El Shaddai, the Father-Mother God—proved sufficient for everything. The wonder of El Shaddai (the power to create new things in the old world) runs through the whole kingdom of grace. If we think we are going to produce the Son of God in ourselves by prayer or obedience or consecration, we are making exactly the same blunder that Sarah and Abraham made over Hagar. We are born not of the will or of the flesh or of the will of man, but of God. As soon as we realize that the thing is impossible, then God will do it. To be brought to the verge of the impossible is to be brought to the margin of the reservations of God. The Everlasting Yea is reached when we perceive that God is El Shaddai, the All-Sufficient God. So far as God is concerned, there is no need for the years of silence and discipline if we will only hear the everlasting No and not try to make it Yea. God does not discard the old and create something entirely new; He creates something in the old until the old and the new are made one. Because a man who has lived in sin stops sinning, it is no sign that he is born from above. Jesus did not talk about new birth to a sinner, but to a religious man, a godly man full of rectitude. Nicodemus worshiped God as a reminiscence; he had not the creation of El Shaddai in him. The creation of El Shaddai is what is made possible by the Lord Jesus (see Galatians 4:19).

The Reasonableness of the Everlasting Way

Abraham's faith was to be permanent; that is, he must walk continually before the eyes of the Almighty in the conscious unconsciousness of His presence. We won't walk before God because we are not confident in Him, and the proof that we are not confident in God is that occasionally we get into the sulks. If we are walking with God, it is impossible to be in the sulks, for we are walking in the permanent light of faith.

Suppose Job had said, "If I were trusting in God I should not be treated like this." He *was* trusting in God, and he *was* treated like that. Faith is not that we see God, but that we know God sees us. That is good enough for us, and we will run out and play—a life of absolute freedom.

The spiritual sulks arise because we want something other than God; we want God to give us something, to make us feel better, to give us wonderful insight into the Bible. That is not the attitude of a saint, but of a sinner who is trying to be a saint and who is coming to God to get things from Him. Unless we give to God the things we get from Him, they will prove our perdition.

The Rectitude of the Everlasting Day

Abraham was still lacking in the development of his faith and was therefore not yet blameless. Had he stayed in the Land of Promise, he would have been blameless; instead, he went down to Egypt and so was not blameless. We must beware lest we ignore what the old theologians called prevenient grace, that is, receiving beforehand the grace of God which will keep us worshiping Him instead of trusting in our wits. If we put moral wits in the place of mystic worship, we will go wrong every time.

The errors Abraham made, as well as the glorious things he did, have been recorded and traced out for our edification. We are not to follow all the steps of Abraham, but to follow the steps of his faith.

In our own lives we try to scrape off our defects and say, "There, I think I am all right now." That is not walking blamelessly before God, but walking in determined opposition to faith in God. If we walk in faith in God there will be no specks to rub off; but if we don't walk in faith in God, everything is a defect and a stain, however good we are. Imagine anyone who has seen himself in the light of Jesus Christ thinking in terms of his defects! Why, we are too filthy for words! Defects don't begin to describe it. We have the sentence of death in ourselves that we should not trust in ourselves but in God, and there are no specks on God. I have determined to take no one seriously but God, and the first person I have to leave severely alone as being the greatest fraud I have ever known is myself. "Oh, I am sick of myself," you say. If you really were sick of yourself you would go to your own funeral and for ever after let God be all in all. Until you get to that point you will never have faith in God.

"I don't know what to do," you say? Then don't do anything. "I don't see anything." Well, don't look for anything. Be foolish enough to trust in God. According to common sense it is the height of madness to have faith in God. Faith is not a bargain: "I will trust You if You give me something, but not if You don't." Faith is trusting God whether He sends us money or not, whether He gives us health or not. Faith is trusting in God, not in His gifts.

Let us walk before God and be perfect, you in your circumstances and I in mine. Then we will prove ourselves true children of Abraham.

Genesis 17:2–14

Awe

Then Abram fell on his face (17:3).

It is significant to note the times when Abraham did not speak to God but remained silent before Him—not sullen, but silent. Awe is just that—reverential dread and wonder. Beware of its imitation, for the pose of reverential awe is the greatest cloak for unbelief. Awe is the condition of a man's spirit when he realizes who God is and what He has done for him personally. No attitude expresses such solemn awe and familiarity as completely as the attitude of a child.

The Personal Relationship in Faithfulness (17:2)

The covenant with the Father of the Faithful is applicable to every man when once faith (that is, a relationship between the individual and God) is born. Frequently we make covenants with ourselves or with our experiences or with our transactions—"I surrendered to God." These are covenants of self-idolatry, an attempt to consecrate our earnest consecration to God. Our covenant with God is not a question of covenanting to keep our vows before Him; it is a matter of covenanting to keep covenant with God who makes the covenant with us. In the matter of salvation it is God's honor that is at stake, not our honor.

Few of us have faith in God; the whole thing is a solemn vow with our religious selves. We promise that we will do what God wants; we vow that we will remain true to Him, and we solemnly mark a text to this effect. But no human being can do it. We steadily have to refuse to promise anything and give ourselves over to God's promise, flinging ourselves entirely onto Him, which is the only possible act of the faith that comes as God's gift. It is a personal relationship to God's faith—"between Me and thee."

"*Come unto me,*" said Jesus. The thing that keeps us from coming is religious self-idolatry. We will not let God make a covenant with us; instead, we will make vows with Him. Vowing means we can do it if we pledge ourselves to do it (see Exodus 19:8). We have to stake ourselves on the truthfulness of God's character; what He does with us is a matter of indifference. Rather than trusting in our own trust, we must trust in the Lord.

The Profound Realization of Fruition (17:3)

Abraham's posture is an expression of deep humility, trustful confidence, and pure joy—the characteristics of faith in God. Whenever we make a transaction with God, it is real instantly and we have the witness. When there is no witness, no humility, no confidence or joy, it is because we have made a transaction with our religious self, and we say, "I must wait for God's witness." That is self-idolatry; there is no trust in God in it, just the mewling of a sick infant.

Like a child we must fling ourselves clean over onto God and wash our hands of the consequences. Then John 14:27—"My peace I give to you"—becomes true at once. The profound realization of God makes us too unspeakably peaceful to be capable of any self-interest.

The Precious Recognition of Fellowship (17:3–4)

The faith that is the creation of God's Spirit in the human soul is never private and personal. When once that faith is created we are caught up into the terrific universal purpose of God; the Holy Spirit destroys our personal, private life and turns it into a thoroughfare for God. Faith is not the means whereby we take God to ourselves for our exclusive purposes; faith is the gift of God whereby He expresses His purposes through us. God can do with us exactly what He likes without saying a by your leave. He does not ask permission to use us any more than we ask permission to use our hands. However, we have to keep our connections with Him clear. Full power cannot be put into a machine that is out of gear (see 1 John 1:7).

The Promised Royalty of Fatherhood (17:4)

This amazing promise expresses the power of God and the moral hysterics it can produce. When God's purpose begins to dawn in my consciousness, my heart resounds with the laughter of the possibility of the impossible. This is no cynical chuckle of doubt. It is the ringing laughter of belief that the impossible is exactly what God does. The sure sign that we have no faith in God is that we have no faith in the supernatural. No man can believe God unless God is in him. The promises to Abraham are God all over from beginning to end. We don't only make room for God, but believe that God has room enough for us.

The Physical Sign of Spirituality (17:5–14)

The new name "Abraham" announced a new disposition, and the rite of circumcision represented the renewal of the whole into a more noble nature by the presence of a new disposition within (see Matthew 5:48). Circumcision, or sanctification which it symbolizes, is the decision to cut away all self-idolatry and abandon to God entirely. The old nature and the new have to be made one. In the Old Testament, circumcision was the sign that they were one; in the New Testament, sanctification was the sign.

This new creation is made by El Shaddai in the old world. When the Holy Spirit comes in, the two natures are there distinctly, and they have to be amalgamated into one nature. The old has to be turned into a noble nature by the incoming of God; the new disposition is the one in which God is all.

The Judaisers taught that all those who were of the direct historic seed of Abraham were all right. The apostle John said, "No, it is not by physical generation but by supernatural generation" (see John 1:12–13). Then came the spiritualizers who denied that God had anything to do with the physical generation. And again the apostle said, "No. Jesus Christ came that way" (see 1 John 4:2), which was proof that everything that has been defiled is to be made holy through Christ. Beware of insulting God by being a pious prude instead of a pure person.

Genesis 17:15–27

Ecstasy

Then Abraham fell on his face and laughed (17:17).

There are certain phases of the life of faith that look so much like cant and humbug that we are apt to grieve God's Spirit by our religious respectability in regard to them. Ecstasy is one of those phases. An ecstatic man is one whose state of mind is marked by mental alienation from his surroundings as his very consciousness is altered into excessive joy. Such a state can be an open gateway for God or for the Devil. If we are worked up by thrills of our own seeking, they will provide a gateway for the Devil; but when they come unsought in faithful performance of duties, they are the gateway into direct communication with God. Abraham's laughter was just such a gateway.

The Paradoxes of God and Human Emotion
(17:15–16)

Laughter and weeping are the most intense human emotions, and these profound wells are to be consecrated to God. This is the first time laughter is mentioned in the Bible, and it is significant. The promise of God was so great that Abraham sank reverently upon the ground, and so paradoxical that he laughed in ecstasy. This was not doubt, but amazement; the thing was so completely impossible that Abraham believed it

92

absolutely—so absolutely that his equilibrium was upset. We have all experienced such ecstasy in minor degrees. Every time we have transacted business with God and have let go entirely on Him, there is such a complete, overwhelming sense of being His creation that we are transfigured by peace and joy.

Laughter that is not the laughter of a childlike heart right with God can be terrible; it can be the laugh of scorn or ridicule or delight in evil. Such laughter is as the crackling of burning thorns. But the laughter of the joy-filled child of God is a delight to behold.

The Princess of God in Human Expression (17:17)

Sarah means "princess," probably referring to her position as "*mother* of nations." This name was not earned by Sarah, but was conferred because of the new thing created in her by her faith in God. When we find unfortunate characteristics in Abraham and Sarah, and in ourselves, we have to realize that God's designations refer to what He redemptively creates in us. The treasure is "in earthen vessels."

A princess in God's sense is not a princess when she prides herself on her own initiative. When our Lord says, "the same is My sister and mother," note the condition of His designation: "whosoever shall do the will of My Father which is in heaven," not whosoever has done the will of God once. Faith is a fountain of living water overflowing. If we keep living the life of faith, then we shall be a sister or brother of the Lord Jesus. There is only one way to live the life of faith, and that is to *live it*.

The Purpose of God and Human Expectation (17:18–21)

Abraham had been contented with the supposition that Ishmael was the child of promise, but in this new revelation from God he learns that the true heir is yet to be born. In fact,

God even tells Abraham the exact time of the child's birth. Why does God suddenly get so specific with His promise? Perhaps because until now there had been the mingling of doubt with Abraham's faith; until now he had not trusted God completely because he did not see how He was going to fulfill His word.

The Program of God and Human Exercise (17:22–27)

These verses show how thoroughly Abraham obeyed God in carrying out the prescribed rite of circumcision. God used circumcision (as He did the rainbow) as a sign and symbol of His promise. Circumcision became for the historic people of God a real sign of the covenant with Him, a sign that they were His people. God had made a covenant promise to them, but He needed a sign of their agreement. They gave this in the representative act of circumcision.

"For with the heart one believes unto righteousness, and with the mouth confession is made unto salvation," says Romans 10:10. This speaks of the kind of physical representation we make in affirming our faith in Him, the sign that we are His children. For example, the physical act of kneeling in penitence has a more emphatic meaning than we imagine. Perhaps this is why human nature protests such exertions: "But it is so humiliating." Of course it is! The thing that keeps you from obeying is the domination of natural human pride that will not bow to God. Salvation will never be actual until you physically commit yourself to it.

Genesis 18:1–15

Friend of God

"My Lord, if I have now found favor in Your sight, do not pass on by Your servant" (18:3).

The apostle James called Abraham "the friend of God." However, we must never confuse "Savior" with "friend." Our Lord said, "You are My friends," to His disciples, not to sinners. Friendship with God means that there is now something of the nature of God in a man on which God can base His friendship. These qualities are formed by the incoming of the Holy Spirit, not by natural generation. Then, as we obey the revelation granted to us, friendship with God begins, based on the new life created in us. That new life is unutterably humble and holy, unsullied, pure, and absolutely devoted to El Shaddai—the One who creates something *in* the old world and transfigures it.

Friendship with God is faith in action in relation to God and to our fellow men. We love others as God has loved us, and we see in the ingratitude of others the ingratitude we have exhibited to God. The fellowship that arises out of such a friendship is a delight to the heart of God.

The Altar of Fellowship (18:1–15)

This manifestation of God to Abraham is the most striking sign in the old covenant of the Incarnation. The Incarnation in practical identification means the manifestation of God in mortal flesh in every detail of human life. Our Lord was not an ascetic like John the Baptist; He was not limited or proscribed and fanatical. In our Lord's life the natural and the supernatural were reconciled; the natural was not violently discarded.

There was no ostensible preparation for the coming of the Son of God. It was only when the surgery of events had taken place that their eyes were opened and they knew Him. Our Lord comes in the most casual way, and we will miss Him unless our nature is prepared to discern Him. The most amazing evidence of a man's nature being changed is the way in which he sees God. To say "God led me here" or "God spoke to me" is an everyday occurrence to him and as natural as speech.

The altar of fellowship means that in every occurrence of life we offer ourselves in devotion to God. Abraham had difficulty at first in bringing the actual details of his life into touch with his real faith in God. In contrast, our Lord's actual life was a continual manifestation of His real faith in God; every detail—whether it was washing His disciples' feet, fasting, praying, or celebrating marriage feasts—manifested the altar of fellowship.

The Discipline of Fellowship (18:6–8)

The reality of God being our guest is the most awe-ful joy in the discipline of fellowship. The spirit of hospitality is such that in or with the stranger we receive the Lord Himself. Abraham served God as he would have served the stranger coming to his door. This revealed his essential readiness for God.

We cannot dress ourselves up, put on behavior that is not ours and moods that have nothing to do with our true nature, and expect to offer God suitable accommodation. The only way in which we can have God as our guest is by receiving from Him the Holy Spirit who will turn our bodies into His home. It is not that we prepare a palace for God; rather, He comes into our mortal flesh and we do our ordinary work, in an ordinary setting, among ordinary people, as we would do it for Him. Our Lord teaches that we have to receive those He sends as though receiving Him (see Matthew 10:40). Therefore, when we receive hospitality from others in His name, we have to remember that it is being offered to our Master, not to us. Somehow it is easier to receive the rebuffs and the spurnings than to receive the hospitality and welcome really offered to our Lord. We say, "But I cannot accept this." If we are to be identified with our Lord, we will have to go through the humiliation of accepting things of which we feel ourselves unworthy.

Times of feasting reveal a man's master like nothing else in human life, and it was in those times that our Lord revealed Himself to be Master. In like manner, our treatment of Jesus Christ is revealed in the way we eat and drink. If we are gluttons, we put Him to shame; if we are ascetics, we refuse to fellowship with Him. But when we become humble saints, we honor Him and celebrate with Him in the ordinary ways of daily life.

The Lord's Supper is a symbol of what we should be doing all the time. It is not a memorial of One who has gone, but of One who is always here. "This do in remembrance of Me" says that we should be in such fellowship with Him that we show His death until He manifests Himself again. He chose the common bread and wine to show us that the evidence of the discipline of fellowship takes place in the common elements and events of life.

The Illumination of Fellowship (18:9–15)

Abraham's laughter was the joyful laughter of faith. Sarah's laughter was the questioning laughter of doubt. She had yet to come to the place where her faith was as active as Abraham's, where she was certain that what God had said would happen, would happen.

There are times when God seems to overlook certain forms of unbelief, and there are other times when He brings our unbelief out suddenly into the light and makes us cringe with shame before it. Not because He wants to show how miserable and mean we are, but because our particular form of doubt is hindering the expression of His purpose in and through us.

A child of faith must never limit the promise of God by what seems good to him, but must give to the power of God the preference over his own reason. God never contradicts reason; He always transcends it. We limit God by remembering what we have allowed Him to do for us in the past; this hinders God and grieves His Spirit. In a time of communion God brings to us a real illumination of His word and we feel thoroughly exhilarated; then we begin to bring in our "buts."

In verses 9–14 we find a record of the most remarkable table-talk in the world: the table-talk of God with Abraham and Sarah. It gives evidence of the ease of their fellowship. The Lord asks, "Why did Sarah laugh?" When Sarah tries to deny it, He gently but firmly rebukes her, "No, but you did laugh!"

Whenever we are rebuked by God for indulgence in unbelief, we should take it as an honor, because prompt obedience on our part will mean the expression of God's purpose in and through us. The things that burden us either make us laugh at their absurdity or make us realize that God is burdening us for His own purpose.

Genesis 18:16–33

Getting There

But Abraham still stood before the LORD. And Abraham came near and said . . . (18:22, 23).

Abraham came into intimate relationship with God without impertinence or lack of reverence. The meaning of intercession is that we see what God is doing and as a result there is an intimacy between the child and the Father that is never impertinent. We can pour into the bosom of God the cares that give us pain and anxiety in order that He may solve for us, and before us, the difficulties we cannot solve. We injure our spiritual life when we simply dump the whole thing down before God and say, "You do it." That is not real union with God. Instead, we must dump ourselves down in the midst of our problems and watch God solve them for us. "But I have no faith," you may say. Bring your problems anyway; then stay with God while He solves them, and God Himself and the solution of your problems will be forever your own.

If we could see the floor of God's immediate presence, we would find it strewn with the "toys" of God's children who have said, "This is broken. I can't play with it any more. Please give me another present." Only one in a thousand sits down in the midst of it all and says, "I will watch my Father mend this and see how He does it." God must not be treated as a hospital for our broken toys, but as our Father.

The Actual and Real in Union (18:16–19)

Abraham sees Jehovah, but he also does his duty to his guests; he does not forget the courtesy of seeing his sublime visitors on their way as if they were ordinary men. Such union of the actual and the real was an habitual condition in the life of our Lord. It is not so with us until we learn to make it so, as Abraham did. We have a wonderful time of communion with God; then comes the spiritual pout: "I have to go and clean boots . . . or write an essay!" Beware of the tendency to wish that God would pretend you are someone special. It is a childish make-believe, standing on spiritual tiptoe to look as big as God: "Others can do this and that, but I must give myself to prayer." The great secret of the obedient life of faith is that the actual conditions of bodily life are transfigured by real communion with God.

In verse 17 notice the communing of God with Himself before He gives the revelation to Abraham. God cannot reveal Himself to just anyone; the revelations of God are determined by the condition of individual character (see Psalm 18:24–26). God takes up the man who is worthy to be the recipient of a revelation. Abraham by his own obedience was such a man, and God brought him into union with Himself—not into absorption, but into complete union.

The Awful Reckoning (18:20–22)

The outcry against Sodom and Gomorrah is the moral outcry against sin, demanding its punishment. Every grain of sand cries out for the punishment of sin (see Genesis 4:10). Only a few human beings echo this cry in intercession—those who know God.

"I will know" whether they are guilty, says God. This is the introduction of the final decision: has the limit of the long-suffering patience of God been reached (18:22)? "The men" referred to in this verse must be connected with verse 1 of the next chapter. They are the two angels who accompanied Jehovah, and in the form of men they depart to introduce the final test. They depart, but Abraham "still stood before the LORD."

The Appealing Reverence to the Uttermost
(18:23–33)

There is no impertinence in Abraham's attitude, only profound humility and intense intimacy. Abraham is not questioning God, but bringing himself to see how God will solve the matter. God allows Abraham to come out with his full intercession until Abraham begins to grasp the essential conditions by which God governs all things. Abraham goes on from step to step, and Jehovah grants him each step, without once going before his request. The stopping point is reached by reason of the fact that Abraham was in complete communion with God throughout the progress of his intercession. After the final test, prayer is impossible (see 1 John 5:16).

By means of intercession we understand more and more the way God solves the problems produced in our minds by the conflict of actual facts and our real faith in Him. Whenever temptations contend in our minds or things meet us in the providence of God that seem to involve a contradiction of what we believe, let the conviction of God's righteousness remain unshaken.

It is an insult to sink before God and say "Thy will be done" when there has been no intercession. That is the prayer of impertinent unbelief. We might as well say, "There is no use in praying; God does whatever He chooses anyway."

The saying "Thy will be done" is born of the most intimate relationship to God wherein we talk to Him freely. In Abraham's prayer there is a distinction between the begging that knows no limit and the prayer that is conscious there are limits set by the holy character of God. Repetition in intercessory importunity is not bargaining, but the joyous insistence of prayer.

The nearer Abraham came to God in his intercession, the more he recognized his entire unworthiness: "Indeed now, I who *am but* dust and ashes have taken it upon myself to speak to the Lord." Genuine unworthiness is never shy before God, any more than a child is shy before its mother. The child of God is conscious only of his or her entire dependence upon God.

In the beginning of our spiritual life our prayers are not of faith but of fretfulness. But I defy you to go on praying for yourself when you get into the inner place. It never occurs to you to do so because you have been brought into relationship with God who makes your spirit partake of His own. Whenever our Lord spoke of importunity in intercession it was never for ourselves but for others. When by imperceptible degrees we stop praying for ourselves, we are "getting there." Prayer is the supreme activity of all that is noblest in our personality, and the essential nature of prayer is faith.

Genesis 19:1–29

Scarcely Saved

> So it came to pass, when he had brought them outside, that
> he said, "Escape for your life! Do not look behind you nor
> stay anywhere in the plain. Escape to the mountains, lest
> you be destroyed" (19:17).

God has given us a precious gift in that we can look at
other Christians and see not them, but the Lord. If we see only
where others are *not* the Lord, it is we who are wrong, not
they. If we can see nothing of God in others, it is because He is
not in us. When we get on our moral high horse, we begin
twisting Christian humility into Pharisaism; we mistake suspi-
cion for discernment. When we are right with God on the
basis of His redemption, however, and we then see some things
in others that are not of God, it is in order that God may
restore them through our intercession. Such chapters as this
and the previous one enable us to understand the essential
nature of this intercession and of God's redemption.

Prepared by Gracious Experiences (19:1–3)

The manifestation given to Lot corresponds to that given
to Abraham in the previous chapter (18:2). Lot was not a
noble man of God like Abraham, but the fact that he bowed
himself to the ground before the angels shows that he retained

103

the power to know when God was near. In comparison with his generation, Lot was righteous, and his contact with Abraham had its effect. Such preparation by gracious experiences occurs in our personal lives, and these experiences should be cherished, for they enable us to do the right thing when we might otherwise do wrong. Beware of not heeding the angel of God in whatever form he comes to you.

In verse 3 it says that the angels entered Lot's house. The entrance of God into a house does not secure anything, but reveals that there is something there with which God has affinity. It is never our merit God looks at, but our faith. If there is only one strand of faith among all the corruption within us, God will take hold of that one strand.

After every temptation, notice where your affinities lie. If you have gone through the temptation successfully, your affinities will be with the highest and purest (see Matthew 4:11). But if you have not the affinity with the highest, it is a sign that your spiritual susceptibilities have become blunted. The seal of doom in a man is that he cannot believe in purity, and this can only be accounted for by an internal twist. What is true in individual lives had become appallingly true in Sodom.

Proposals of Great Evil (19:4–9)

The history of Sodom reveals that sin is the beginning of the most appalling corruption. Sin is a disposition, not a deed; and the corruption of Sodom was the result of sin. Because this distinction between what we are apt to call sin and what the Bible calls sin has been lost, pseudo-evangelical preaching has maintained that only moral blackguards need fear the judgment of God. Yet our Lord seemed to be infinitely sterner with the moral, upright Pharisees than with the sinful publicans (see Matthew 21:31). He looked at something we cannot see, and that is the disposition.

Lot was the only one who stood as a representative of God in Sodom, and while he was free from the abominations of Sodom, he was not far from its worldly mind. Because of this, he panicked, and panic always advocates doing wrong that right may result. In fact, this tendency to *do* instead of to devote one's self to God is nearly always the sign of a smudged relationship to God.

Lot's was the doubting heart that soon turns to double ways. This was because Lot borrowed most of his piety (12:4). Such sentimental spirituality chooses the visible things instead of Him who is invisible, and slowly and surely this weak faith settles down between mammon and righteousness. In the supreme test, Lot trusted his wits, whereas Abraham worshiped and waited.

Performance of God's Ends (19:10–29)

Abraham, standing alone with God, was the key to the rescue of Lot and his family. In answer to Abraham's intercession, the angels pulled them out of Sodom, ready or not. Yet Lot was rescued with the greatest difficulty because of his vacillation, which led to fear and impaired judgment. Vacillation in a crisis is the sign of an unabandoned nature. An abandoned nature cannot vacillate because there is nothing to weigh; it is completely abandoned to God.

When we do not come in contact with God for ourselves, difficulties soon wall us in like fire. Afraid to move this way or that, we watch our own steps rather than the path of God. Our only escape is rescue, and God does that by means of the intercession of others. When this happens, we must beware of accepting His way of escape as some blessing or vision granted as an indication of our goodness. It owes nothing to us, and all to the mercy and purpose of God.

Genesis 19:30–38

Wrecked in Harbor

Then Lot went up out of Zoar and dwelt in the mountains
. . . for he was afraid to dwell in Zoar. And he and his two
daughters dwelt in a cave (19:30).

One would think that the person who has passed through
great storms and made harbor should be safe. Yet some, like
Lot, become shipwrecked in harbor on the shoal of spiritual
cleverness.

"Cleverness," said Sir James Paget, "is a character of mind
the exercise of which is so instantly and pleasantly rewarded,
that the temptation to cultivate it is always present." He was
speaking of intellectual cleverness, but we can make the same
application to the spiritual. We may not have much mental
cleverness, but some of us are dexterously clever spiritually.
For example, we deliberately "loaf," living on the memories of
the times when God came in and did the thing—only we call it
"relying on the Holy Ghost." There are times when God does
give real spiritual insight and times when He does not; but if
between the times of inspiration we do not work but loaf, we
are leading up to tremendous failure one day. The moments of
light and inspiration are a standard; if we let down in the times
between those moments, trusting in our own spiritual cleverness, we shall fail.

The Natural History of the Prudent Peril

The sinful prudence which appeared in the life of Abraham (12:10) appeared again in the lives of his kindred, and was the persisting defect in Lot's character. A man's actions do not end with himself. He may not see the cumulative effect, but later generations will. The prudence peril began with Adam and passed on to Noah, then Abraham, and on to Lot and others until it became the most dominant characteristic of Israel and Judah. The terror of the prudence peril is that it can end in a deed such as Lot's. "But I never could do such things," you say. What one man has done, any man can do if he does not heed that which is given for our instruction.

The error is putting prudence in competition with God's will—weighing pros and cons before God when He has already spoken. When you want other people to commend the decision you have made, it is an indication that you have trusted your wits instead of worshiping God. If you say, "But I can prove I was right," you may be sure you are wrong, because you have to use your own ingenuity to prove you are right. When you act in faith in God, it is not logical proof that you are right that matters, but the certainty of Divine approval, and this keeps you from seeking the approval of others. We must use our wits to *assist* us in worshiping God and carrying out His will, not in carrying out our own will and then piously asking God to bless the concoction. Rely on God to direct you in choosing according to His will, not on your own wits. Worship first, wits second.

The Natural History of Panic Perversity

Sensual passion always follows spent panic. It is easy to fall into the sins of the flesh when the ideals of life lose their power. All you have to do is to get into a panic about something and you will give the Devil opportunity to have perverse power over your body.

Panic was entirely absent from the life of our Lord; conse-quently He had nothing of the nature of perversity. Notice how our Lord continually curbed the impulsive Peter. He knew that impulse is apt to lead to panic, and panic opens the door to perversity and sensuality. A saint has no right to give way to a panic of nerves, for if we do, we give the temple of the Holy Ghost over to the Devil. On the borders of hysteria lurk all the demons that can clutch and possess human nature.

Few of us realize the power we can truly have over the emotions—or the power emotions can exert over us, if we do not bring them under the control of the Holy Ghost. An emo-tion allowed sway on one level, seemingly innocent because it does not manifest itself in action, will soon descend to the next lower level, and so on, until we are acting it out in all its perverse reality. God's Word is rugged and unvarnished on this point: our Lord requires not only chastity of body, but chastity of thought.

Genesis 20:1–7

Philistinism

And Abraham journeyed from there to the South, and dwelt between Kadesh and Shur, and stayed in Gerar (20:1).

The term "philistinism" owes its popularity to Matthew Arnold and is used today in reference to uncultured people. We use it here because this is the first meeting of the house of Abraham with the Philistines, and also because at this stage Abraham lapsed into confidence in himself and into compromise with spiritually uncultured people—that is, those who did not know the ways of Jehovah.

To say "I can't understand how Abraham could do this" is self-deception. If you will truly look inside your own heart, you will never say such a thing. We have to be careful lest we blind ourselves by putting up our own standards instead of the standards of God. When we put God's standard up, that is, God Himself, there is no room for personal vanity. It is self-deception to say, "Because I am saved and sanctified all I do is sure to be right." As long as we establish ourselves or even some revered saint as the standard of righteousness, we will be blinded by complacency.

Only the grace of God makes us honest with ourselves and our own shallow tricks, no matter what our profession of Christianity. We are so altogether perverse that God Almighty had to come and save us! Whenever we forget this and begin to set up little standards of our own, imbedded in some favorite saint, we are sure to go wrong. We have to get rid of all notions about ourselves and our own standards and keep before us our Lord Himself. Then we will not be tempted to delusion about ourselves. Our eye must be on God, not on ourselves.

The Disposition of Reaction (20:1)

When the Bible records facts of experience, look in your own experience for the answer; when the Bible reveals standards of revelation, look to God, not to experience.

After a state of great spiritual excitement, Abraham, as on a former occasion (see chapter 12), decides to change his residence. If we bring the light of experience to this reaction on the part of Abraham, we shall understand how even such a believer as he fell the second time into the same sin. We are apt to say, "I won't do that thing again now that God has warned me." But you will. You will do it as certainly as Abraham did if you trust to your vows instead of to God.

Always beware when you are perfectly certain you are right, so certain that you do not dream of asking God's counsel. Our confidence rests not with our wits, but with God. We must never depend on our own moral judgment or our intellectual discernment or our sense of right and justice. All these are right in themselves, but not right in us; we can only be right as we remain absolutely confident in God.

When we realize that we have repeated a sin, the danger is to lie down in the mud and refuse to get up. There is no refuge in vowing or in praying; there is refuge in only one place, in absolute, childlike confidence in God.

The Discretion of Reason (20:2)

From any standpoint it would seem Abraham was doing the right thing in getting away from Sodom; it would seem the act of a wise, sensible, reasoning man of God. But Abraham was not God's man in going because as soon as he does, God rebukes him. In going to Gerar, as in going down to Egypt, Abraham thought he was justified; but in each case the results are entirely different from what he intended—in each case Sarah is taken from him. Whenever we base a decision on our ordinary wisdom, we can injure others, as well as our relationship to God. Abraham had no notion that he was doing wrong to Abimelech, but the record proves that he did, and also that he injured his relationship to God. The only safeguard is dependence upon God, not on godly decisions.

"I know I am right," we say, claiming the superiority of our logical moral right. And it has to be proved to us that from the standpoint of the Holy Ghost we are wrong. If I can prove to my own mind that I am right, by that very act I am wrong in my disposition toward God.

The Dream of Realization (20:3)

The fact that God makes good come out of my wrong does not make my wrong right. I have simply used God's permissive will to go in a circle when I should have gone straight. There are times when you see what God wants and you begin to obey with the simple, direct obedience of a child. Then come the choppy waters of friends' advice or of your own considerations, and for a while you toss around because you have become discreet and shrewd and wise instead of being a child of God. After the passing of days, or longer, depending on your stubbornness, God brings you out of all the turmoil, and the Devil comes and says it was a good thing after all. It was not; it was a bad thing. You prevented God's order being worked out directly through you, and He had to allow you to go in a circle.

Beware of justifying yourself when God alone is the justifier. If ever I can justify myself, I make God unjust. If I am right and morally based in all I do and say, I do not need a Savior, and God is not justified in the extravagant waste of sending Jesus Christ to die for me. If God judges me a sinner who needs saving, and I can prove that I am just, I make God unjust. When I uphold myself in any way, be I saint or sinner, it is a blow in the face of God and is a proof that I am wrong. If in any detail I take the justice of God and make it mean my own justice, I thereby prove God to be unjust. This is part of the mystery of godliness and can only be understood by the intuition of faith (see Matthew 11:25).

The Dilemma of Rectitude (20:4–7)

It is God who engineers circumstances. Every time Abraham refused to see this, every time he stepped in and relied on himself to engineer circumstances, he upset everything.

Out of His sheer mercy, God stepped in and kept Abimelech from sinning. There is a difference between deliverance from sin by God's sovereign act, which is an occasion for praise, and the defiance of sin by personal integrity, which results in the building up of character. There are times in our lives when God by a sovereign act prevented us from committing sin; and when we look back and see how He preserved us, the danger is to say it must have been because of our innocence or our own morality. No, it was the mercy of God.

Genesis 20:8–18

Humiliation

And Abraham said, "Because I thought, surely the fear of God *is* not in this place, and they will kill me on account of my wife" (20:11).

Humiliation and humility must not be confused. Humility can never be humiliated. When applied to our Lord, humiliation does not refer at all to His personal caliber, but to the lowering of His external form from "being in the form of God" to "taking the form of a servant." As applied to us, humiliation means a lowering of our prideful condition in some way. Whenever we pride ourselves on anything as being of real acceptance to God and then realize that He absolutely ignores that thing, we experience the humbling of humiliation.

The Humility and Honor of Abimelech (20:8–10)

Abimelech's true humility is revealed in the way he communicates the events of his dream to his servants; he deliberately makes known before his whole court the compromising position in which he has been placed. His confession is intensely public, and his confrontation with Abraham rigorous, yet not vindictive—although there is stinging irony in what he says to Sarah (20:8–11, 16).

In nine cases out of ten, reserve is simply personal pride, which will turn to insolence or iniquity at a moment's notice.

One of the most delicate issues in the history of the human soul is that of concealing what ought to be made known and of making known what ought to be concealed. When concealing is a great relief, question it; when revealing is a great relief, question it. The only guiding factor is obedience to the highest we know—at all cost. The wriggling we indulge in to escape from being humiliated prevents our being right with God. For instance, we have a wrong attitude of mind toward another, and the Spirit of God tells us to put it right (see Matthew 5:24), and we say, "No, I will just put it right between myself and God." We cannot do it; it is impossible. Instead of deliberately obeying God, irrespective of what it costs, we try to use prayer to cover our own cowardice; it is a subtle subterfuge to prevent ourselves being humiliated.

It was an attitude of independence from God on the part of Abraham that brought trouble on the house of Abimelech. Abraham repeated the mistake he had made with Pharaoh because of a wrong attitude toward God. Abimelech had reason to complain about the conduct of Abraham in the same way that Pharaoh had reason to complain of it (12:13-20), and Abimelech did not shrink from declaring his injured sense of truth and justice. Imagine Abraham's humiliation when he realized what he had done.

The Humiliation and Honor of Abraham (20:11–18)

The way in which Abraham offers his apologies reveals clearly that he was ashamed. The fear of man that had driven him earlier was awakened afresh by what he had so recently seen in Sodom, and he was suspicious of human nature everywhere. Abraham ashamedly explains his motive and his equivocation (20:11). He admits that Sarah is not his sister, but he also indicates that his reason for lying has deservedly brought him humiliation. There was none of the sneaky element in Abraham that we see later in Jacob; Abraham was trying to guard Sarah for God because of the promised child.

We are always in danger of mistaking personal predilections for Christian perfection, and we have to learn to take the veil off our moral quirks. Over and over again it works like this: we begin to be cunning and think, "Now, if I am not careful that man will use my position for his own purposes." The real reason we say it is that we do not like that particular man and imagine, therefore, that God does not like him either. Just the reverse can be true if it is a person we like. It is the same old trick of leaning on our own understanding and trying to work out God's order in our own way, instead of allowing God to carry out His order in His own way.

Our Lord never evidenced the slightest sign of fear or cunning or diplomacy. He was never suspicious of anyone; yet He trusted in no one except His Father. Consequently He was never vindictive, nor was He ever humiliated. It is only possible to be humiliated when we are serving our own pride.

Abraham's defects are clear and his sins obvious, but his nobility is extraordinary. Phases of his life may be used as a type of sanctification, but Abraham himself is a living example of the life of faith with both its failures and its successes. Sanctification is not something our Lord does in us; sanctification is *Himself* in us. "But of Him you are in Christ Jesus, who became for us wisdom from God—and righteousness and sanctification and redemption" (1 Corinthians 1:30).

Genesis 21:1–8

God Is Good

And the LORD visited Sarah as He had said, and the LORD did for Sarah as He had spoken (21:1).

One of the greatest demands on the human spirit is to believe that God is good when His providence seems to prohibit the fulfillment of what He has promised. The one character in the Bible who sustains this strain grandly is Abraham. Paul, in summing up the life of Abraham, points to this as his greatest quality: "Abraham believed God."

God's Performance of His Own Promise (21:1)

No one can fulfill a promise but the one who makes it. These words contain the whole autobiography of the godly ups and downs of the life of faith. During the years when everything seemed to contradict the fulfillment of the promise, Abraham continually forgot this fundamental fact and tried to help God keep His promise. God alone can fulfill His promises, and we have to come to the place of perfect reliance upon God to do just that (see 1 Thessalonians 5:23–24).

Just as the Lord visited Sarah "as He had said," He visits the believer with the word of promise and visits him again with the word of fulfillment. Abraham endured for twenty-five years without any sign of fulfillment. The majority of us

116

know nothing about waiting; we don't wait, we endure. Faithful waiting means that we go on in the perfect certainty of God's goodness—no dumps or fears.

God's Presentation of His Own Performance (21:2)

The presentation of God's performance here is in the birth of an ordinary child, extraordinary only to the eye of faith. We come to God not with faith in His goodness but with a conception of our own, and we look for God to come to us in that way. God cannot come to us in our way; He can only come in His own way—in ways man would never dream of looking for Him. In the Incarnation the eternal God was so majestically small that the world never saw Him. And this is still true today. We cry out, "Oh God, I wish You would come to me," when He is there all the time. Then suddenly we see Him and say, "Surely the Lord is in this place, and I knew it not." We expect desolation and anguish; instead there is laughter and hilarity when we see God. This astonishment at the performance of God is brought out over and over again until we learn to be humiliated at our despicable disbelief.

God's Program for His Progeny (21:3–8)

What Abraham did for his son Isaac was in accordance with God's program for him, not his own. God has a distinct program for every child born into this world. There is no relation between the promise of God for the life He forms in us by regeneration and our personal, private ambitions; those ambitions are completely transfigured. We must heed the promise of God and see that we do not try to make God's gift fulfill our own ends.

Suppose that God sees fit to put us into desolation when He begins the forming of His Son in us. What ought it to matter? All He is after in you and me is the forming of His Son in us. When He drives the sword through the natural, we begin to whine and say, "Oh, I can't go through that"; but we must go through it. If we refuse to make our natural life obedient to the Son of God in us, the Son of God will be put to death in us. We have to put on the new man in our human nature to fit the life of the Son of God in us, and see that in the outer courts of our bodily lives we conduct our life for Him.

Sarah's hilarity is the joy of God sounding through the upset equilibrium of a mind that scarcely expected the promise to be fulfilled (21:6). The son of Sarah is himself a type of the Son of Mary, and in each case the promise is limited through a particular woman, and through an apparently impossible, yet actual birth. Fancy making everything depend on that haughty, inclined-to-be-unstable, not-amazingly-superb-in-rectitude Sarah! How haphazard God seems—not sometimes but always. God's ways turn man's thinking upside down.

Amazement comes when God's promise is fulfilled (21:7). What is known as the dark side of Christian experience is not really Christian experience at all; it is God putting the rot of sacramental death through the natural virtues in order to produce something in keeping with His Son, and all our whining and misery ought to be the laughter of Sarah: "Now I see what God wants!" Instead of that, we moon in corners and gloom before God and say, "I am afraid I am not sanctified."

If we fight against the desolation, we will kill the life of God in us; yield to it, and God's fulfillment will amaze us. It is in the periods of desolation that the sickly pietists talk about "What I am suffering!" They are in the initial stages and have not begun to realize God's purpose. God is working out the manifestation of the fulfillment of His promise, and when it is fulfilled there is never any thought of self or of self-consideration anywhere.

Genesis 21:9–21

Which?

But God said to Abraham, "Do not let it be displeasing in your sight because of the lad or because of your bondwoman. Whatever Sarah has said to you, listen to her voice; for in Isaac your seed shall be called. Yet I will also make a nation of the son of the bondwoman, because he *is* your seed" (21:12–13).

The dilemmas of our personal life with God are few if we obey and many if we are willful. Spiritually the dilemmas arise from the disinclination for discipline; every time I refuse to discipline my natural self, I become less and less of a person and more and more of an independent, impertinent individual. Individuality is the characteristic of the natural man; personality is the characteristic of the spiritual man. That is why our Lord can never be defined in terms of individuality, but only in terms of personality. Individuality is the characteristic of the child; it is the husk of the personal life. It separates and isolates; personality can merge and be blended. The shell of individuality is God's created covering for the protection of the personal life, but individuality must go in order that the personal life may be brought out into fellowship with God—"that they may be one, even as We are one."

The Offense of the Natural (21:9–10)

When Sarah sees the mocking of Ishmael, she begs Abraham to send the boy and his mother away—to cast them out. Somehow Sarah seems to have forgotten that it was she who gave Hagar to Abraham in the first place. We always become anxious when we take our own self-chosen ways. In his epistle to the Galatians the apostle Paul makes his great revelation regarding that which is "born after the flesh" and that which is "born after the Spirit." He is dealing not with sin, but with the relationship between the natural and the spiritual. The natural must be disciplined and turned into the spiritual by sacrifice (see Galatians 5:24), otherwise it will produce a tremendous divorce in the life.

Why did God make it necessary for the natural to be sacrificed to the spiritual? God did not. God's order was that the natural should be transformed into the spiritual by obedience; sin made it necessary for the natural to be sacrificed to the spiritual, and that after sanctification. We have the idea that sanctification means deliverance from sin only; it means much more, however. It means that we start on a life of discipline.

The offense of the natural is its robust ridicule of the spiritual, and if the natural is not "cast out," it will not only perish itself but will lead the whole personal life astray. You must discipline yourself now; if you do not, you will ruin your life for God. If the natural is not sacrificed to the spiritual by me, not by God, it will mock at the life of the Son of God in me and produce continual doubt and wavering—always the result of an undisciplined nature. Instead of "I can't," say "I won't," and you have it exactly; it is the Ishmael jeer.

People go wrong spiritually because they stubbornly refuse to discipline themselves physically, mentally, or in any way, and after a time they become that most contemptible and objectionable thing, a pampered man or woman, and their own greatest cause of suffering. There is no suffering to equal the suffering of self-love arising from independent individuality that refuses to submit either to God or to its nobler self.

The Offering of the Natural (21:11–13)

The casting out of Hagar and Ishmael was necessary not only for the line of promise but for the welfare of Ishmael himself. All the problems regarding civilization and organization and the natural virtues arise because we put them on the throne, where they mock the Son of God. These things are the outcome of the natural life and are to be put in subjection, not because they are wrong, but because they are individual protests against the life of the Son of God in us. The natural life is not spiritual; it can only be made spiritual by deliberately casting it out and making it the slave instead of the ruler. Our business is to make independent individuality conform to the Son of God in us, even though that requires us to act severely.

We are apt to deify willfulness and independence and call them strength. What we call strength of will, however, God looks upon as contemptible weakness. The Being with the greatest will was our Lord Jesus Christ, and yet He never exercised His will, at least not as we think of will. His life was one of meekness and submission (see John 5:19, 30). There was nothing independent or willful or self-assertive about our Lord, and He says, "Learn of Me, for I am meek and lowly in heart." Jesus Christ cannot give us a meek and quiet spirit; we have to take this yoke—His yoke—upon ourselves. That is, we deliberately have to discipline ourselves.

The Sermon on the Mount teaches the destruction of individuality and the exaltation of personality. When the personal life is merged with God, it will manifest the characteristics of

God. Individuality never exhibits the characteristics of God, but of the natural—the characteristics of Ishmael, or of Esau, or of Saul of Tarsus—that mock at the meek and lowly Son of God.

What is it that begins to mock in you? "Meek? Do you think I am going to bow my neck to that? Be loyal there, in my home? Obey a passing sentiment that came to me in a prayer meeting?" Cast out the bondwoman and her son—the natural life and all that nourishes it—or they will lead you to ruin. Then God will bring them back into their rightful inheritance. The natural life can only be brought into union by being cast out.

If we do not resolutely cast out the natural, the supernatural can never become natural in us. There are some Christians in whom the supernatural and the natural seem one and the same, and you say, "Well, they are not one with me. I find the natural at loggerheads with the spiritual." This is because you have not gone through the fanatical stage of cutting off the right arm, gone through the discipline of maiming the natural, completely casting it out. It is not a question of praying, but performing. For those who have, God has brought the natural back into its right relationship, with the spiritual on top; the spiritual manifests itself in a life which knows no division into sacred and secular.

The Ostracism of the Natural (21:14)

It was necessary for Abraham to cast out Hagar and Ishmael, but he did not divorce Hagar. Divorce has to do with apostasy. We must be divorced from sin, not separated from sin, for sin belongs to hell and the Devil. I, as a child of God, belong to heaven and God, and I must have nothing to do with sin in any shape or form. The casting out of Hagar and Ishmael represents the separation that goes on throughout the life of faith: "Present your bodies a living sacrifice"—go to the funeral of your own independence. It is not a question of divorcing myself from something, as I must with sin, but of giving up my right to myself, my natural independence and self-assertiveness.

"If any man will be My disciple, let him deny himself," Jesus says—that is, deny his right to himself; and a man has to realize who Jesus Christ is before he will do it. It is the things that are right and noble and good from the natural standpoint that keep us from God's best. To discern that the natural virtues antagonize surrender to God is to begin to see where the battle lies. It is going to cost the natural everything, not something.

The Ordeal of the Natural (21:15–18)

Beware of blaspheming the Creator by calling the natural sinful. The natural is not sinful, but un-moral and un-spiritual. It is the home of all the vagrant vices and virtues, and must be disciplined with the utmost severity until it learns its true position in the providence of God. Remember, Abraham had to offer up Ishmael before he offered up Isaac.

Some of us are trying to offer spiritual sacrifices before we have sacrificed the natural. The only way we can offer a spiritual sacrifice to God is to do what He tells us to do, discipline what He tells us to discipline. Under no circumstances can we dictate to God on the basis of the natural life. When God's Son tells me to do a thing, I have no business to allow the natural to dictate and say, "I cannot do that because I get so tired." What does it matter if it kills the natural? God's purpose for the natural will be fulfilled if I do not make God wait on my natural inclinations.

The Outrance of the Natural (21:19–21)

Outrance—the utmost extremity or bitter end. That was where Ishmael found himself—in the wilderness. Yet "God was with the lad." After Ishmael had learned by experience that he was not a fellow heir with Isaac, he was richly endowed by Abraham; he also remained in friendly relationship with Isaac (25:9).

When we put our natural life out in the desert, resolutely cast it out and keep it under, then God is with it; He opens up wells and oases and fulfills His promise for it. It requires stern discipline and rigorous severity to the last degree (see 1 Corinthians 9:27), but when we comply, God will be with the natural life and bring it to its full purpose.

Genesis 21:22–34

Conditions

Thus they made a covenant at Beersheba. . . . Then *Abra-ham* planted a tamarisk tree in Beersheba, and there called on the name of the LORD (21:32, 33).

The life of faith as portrayed in the life of Abraham is a detailed presentation of its majesties and its muddles. We have detected Abraham's blunders when he tried using his own wits, but we must not forget that by far the most striking thing about Abraham is his worship of God.

In this chapter he exhibits the right relationship between common sense and faith. Common sense is not faith and faith is not common sense; they are like Ishmael and Isaac, like the natural and the spiritual, like individuality and personality, like impulse and inspiration. Faith in antagonism to common sense is fanaticism, and common sense in antagonism to faith is rationalism. Only the life of faith brings the two into right relationship.

No one can make them one for me; I must do it for myself. And it can only be done by living it out, not by thinking, just as the natural can only be made spiritual in life, not in think-ing. We have the idea that the body, individuality, and the natural life are altogether of the Devil; they are not. They are of God, designed by God, and it is in the human body and in the natural order of things that we have to exhibit our worship of God. The danger is to mistake the natural for the spiritual, making the natural life God instead of worshiping God in the natural life.

There is only one way to find out what the will of God is, and that is by not trying to find out. If you are born again in the Spirit of God, you are in the will of God, and your ordinary, common-sense decisions are God's will for you unless He gives an inner check. When He does, call a halt immediately and wait on Him. Be renewed in the spirit of your mind that you may make out His will in practical living. God's will in my common-sense life is not for me to *accept* conditions and say, "Oh well, it is the will of God," but to *apprehend* them. Doing the will of God is an active thing in my common-sense life.

The Arbitration Between Abraham and Abimelech (21:22–24)

Abimelech does not stand for the sinful, but for the noble and upright and perfectly natural. The blessing of God is recognized by the natural, but never recognized by the sinful. Abimelech stands as the type of civilization with its organizations and culture and good sense. Between the church, which is an organism, and organization, which is pagan, there must be arbitration. Much of our organization in the church is pagan, and it is our salvation to see this. As soon as we forget this and compromise instead of arbitrate, we have sold the Son of God to the world.

The attitude of faith to organization is illustrated in our Lord's attitude to Pilate. He did not compromise with Pilate; He arbitrated with him: "You have to decide this matter because God has put you in the position where you must. You stand there on your dignity as proconsul: I stand here on My dignity as Son of God. If you put Me to death as your duty, I go to death because it is My duty." There was no compromise there. "If My kingdom were of this world, then My servants would fight." But there was no fight; there was arbitration, and the reason for it was God's order behind the whole thing.

The Apprehension of Abimelech by Abraham (21:25–26)

Abraham distinguishes clearly between political and private rights in the matter of the well, and now he in his turn administers a rebuke to Abimelech. Abimelech throws back the reproof on the plea that he had not been told that the well had been taken away. This is mere natural shrewdness, and is the ground of their first arbitration. It is instructive to notice that Abraham always takes his rebukes magnificently; he never once shows individuality but always personality.

When first we become spiritual we arbitrate with our bodies until we can say, "I will put the natural into absolute subjection and have no more arbitration" (see 1 Corinthians 9:27). The same thing is taking place in the world today. At present there is arbitration between the children of God and the natural forces of civilization. We arbitrate between the two by recognizing the present claims of each without compromising either. When the Lord Jesus comes again there will be no more arbitration; all the natural forces of civilization will instantly be put in subjection to Him, in the same way that those who enter into the sanctified life deliberately put the natural in themselves in subjection to Jesus Christ. In the meantime there is arbitration, no compromise and no fight, but deliberate arbitration between the two.

As Abimelech rebuked Abraham when he was in the wrong, and Abraham in his turn rebuked Abimelech, so in the same way the children of men from time to time rebuke the children of God, and the children of God rebuke the actions of the children of men. Compromise or unity between them is immoral. Arbitration until He comes is the God-ordained program.

Abimelech represents the worldly man who recognizes the value of having the people of God in the midst of his civilization, although he himself does not intend to become one of them. Our Lord did not pray that His disciples should be taken out of the world, but that they should be kept from the evil of the world (see John 17).

The Agreement of Abraham and Abimelech (21:27–34)

The Old Testament Scriptures always regard the oath as a peculiar sacrament. If you read what the Bible says about vowing, you will see how culpably negligent we are in the way we promise. If we do not fulfill a promise, we damage our moral and spiritual life. It is infinitely better to refuse to promise anything, even in the most superficial relationships, than to promise and not perform. If you make a promise, you must see that it is fulfilled, no matter what it costs you. The glib way we promise is indicative of our slipshod ways, of our laziness and indifference. The word of a natural man is his bond; the word of a saint binds God.

The covenant between Abraham and Abimelech was just such a promise: Abimelech was bound by his word as his bond; Abraham was bound by his relationship to God. By means of this promise, Abraham's faith develops more fully into faith in the eternal truth of Jehovah's covenant (21:33).

Genesis 22:1–3

The Supreme Climb

Then He said, "Take now your son, your only *son* Isaac, whom you love, and go to the land of Moriah, and offer him there as a burnt offering on one of the mountains of which I shall tell you" (22:2).

In the life of Abraham we deal with the failures and the triumphs of the life of faith, and this chapter records the perfecting of the obedience of faith in Abraham. His obedience was reflected not only in his willingness to sacrifice Isaac, but in his readiness to perceive a revelation even when it seemed to contradict what God had previously told him. The very nature of faith is that it must be tried; faith untried is only ideally real, not actually real. Because faith is not rational, it cannot be worked out on the basis of logical reason; it can only be worked out implicitly by living obedience. God proved Abraham's faith by placing him in the most extreme crisis possible, for faith must prove itself by the inward concession of the believer's dearest objects.

The Crucible for Abraham (22:1)

"God tested Abraham." These are startling words, for there is nothing abstract or detached about them. This is God, in His providence of rule and grace, dealing directly with one of His own. God did not further Abraham's spiritual life in spite of his circumstances, but in and by his circumstances. The whole purpose of God was to make Abraham's ideal faith actually real in the life of His servant. God was working for His highest purpose until it and man's highest good became one.

The crucible of testing is placed by God, not by man. It is easy to pass a crude verdict on God if you are not living in touch with Him. If you look at God through the mist of the heat of the crucible, you will say God is cruel. You must go through the heart of the crucible before you have any right to pronounce a verdict. Upon entering the crucible, one might say, "God took away my child because I loved her too much." But after passing through, you will find that you have learned to know God better.

Beware of pronouncing any verdict on the life of faith if you are not living it.

The Concentration of Abraham (22:1)

"Here I am," Abraham said when God called. These words express the greatest application of the human mind. To say "Here I am" when God speaks is only possible if we are in His presence, in the place where we can obey. To understand where I am in the sight of God means not only to listen but to obey promptly. Thus, I can use this as a landmark for sighting my position: whenever I want to debate about doing what I know to be supremely right, I am not in touch with God.

The Command to Abraham (22:2–3)

God's words are blows aimed against the incrustations of natural individual life in order that Abraham's personal faith might be emancipated into fellowship with God. The blows are aimed at individuality because individuality, the home of independence and pride, will not come into fellowship with God. When God is developing the faith of a man, all that must be sacrificed. It is the personality that comes into fellowship with God; that is why faith always works on the personal life (see Job 1:12). If you are not in the crucible yourself, the process seems cruel; but if you are, you know the ecstasy of the chrysalis developing into a butterfly, the joy of being brought into personal fellowship with God.

God commanded Abraham, "Take *now* your son." Not presently, not tomorrow, but now. And Abraham's confidence was so fixed that he obeyed instantly. He did not consult with flesh and blood, his own or anyone else's; he did what God commanded. Immediate obedience to the dictates of the Spirit of God is the response of the faithful soul.

It is extraordinary how we debate with right. We know a thing is right, but we seek excuses for not doing it now. Always beware when you want to confer with your own flesh and blood—that is, your own sympathies, your own insight. These things are based on individuality, not on personal relationship to God, and they are the things that compete with God and hinder our faith. When our Lord is bringing us into personal relationship with Himself, it is always the individual relationships He breaks down. He comes with a sword rap on the husks that will not break, that will not let the life out for God (see Luke 14:26). If you are outside the crucible you will say that Jesus Christ is cruel. But when you are in the crucible, you see that it is a personal relationship with Himself that He is after all the time.

The Climb and Consecration of Abraham (22:2–3)

The mountain of the Lord is the very height of the trial into which God brings His servant. Abraham never questions the cost; his implicit understanding of God so far outreaches his explicit knowledge that he trusts God utterly and climbs the highest height and remains unutterably true to God. This mountain is not a mountain of sacrifice, but the mountain of proof that Abraham loved God supremely.

"So Abraham rose early . . . and went to the place of which God had told him." Oh, the wonderful simplicity of Abraham. For this is the sacrifice of *Abraham*, not of Isaac. God chose the crucible for Abraham, and Abraham made no demur; he went steadily through.

If God has given the command, He will look after everything; your business is to get up and go and trustingly wash your hands of the consequences. If God has made your cup sweet, drink it with grace; if He has made it bitter, drink it in communion with Him.

Genesis 22:3–6

Isolation

Then on the third day Abraham lifted his eyes and saw the place afar off (22:4).

God "tested" Abraham to purify him. In doing so, God lifted Abraham's faith into an understanding of Himself. Abraham's life was a life of faith, and faith in its actual working out has to go through spells of wordless isolation (see Romans 8:26). Testings in the life of faith are not accidents; each is part of a plan, a step in the progress of faith. Beware of confusing the trials of faith with the ordinary disciplines of life, however; many things that we call "trials" are really just the inevitable result of being alive.

The Duty of Diligence (22:3)

Here we see that Abraham "rose early in the morning." This phrase is characteristic not only of men and women in the Bible, but of God Himself. The revelation of God in the Old Testament is that of a working God. Unlike other religions that worship gods who rule in lofty disdain, the true God is one who is both diligent and suffering. The God who reveals Himself to Abraham is One ever intent on the fulfillment of His great designs; and He expects His people to do likewise. If God is diligent, surely we ought to be diligent in doing our duty to Him. Think how patient and how diligent God has been with us! Over and over again He gets us near the point, and then by some petty individual sulk we spoil it all, and He patiently begins all over again. Think of His vision for us: "whiter than snow shine." Has God had to begin all over again from where we left off last time, or have we said, "I will be true to God at all costs, no matter what the isolation"?

The Direction of Duty (22:3)

When Abraham "went to the place of which God had told him," he took the direction of his duty from God's word, not from his own discernment. Our tendency is to water down God's word to suit ourselves. God never fits His word to suit us; He fits us to suit His word. We have to remain true to what we see in those rare moments of discernment; we must walk while we have the light (see John 12:35–36). If we do not, we will obstruct God's purpose in our life. Abraham's life is an illustration of two things: of unreserved surrender to God, and of God's complete possession of a child of His for His own highest ends.

It is never the consecration of our gifts that fits us for God's service. Absorption in practical work is one of the greatest hindrances to discerning the call of God. Unless active work is balanced by a deep, isolated solitude with God, knowledge of God does not grow and the worker becomes exhausted and spent. Our Lord said that the only men He can use in His enterprises are those in whom He has done everything (see Luke 14:26–27, 33); otherwise we serve our own ends all the time. Many begin well, but go off on some doctrine; all their energy is spent furthering a cause rather than Jesus Christ. The direction of duty lies not in doing things for God, but in doing what God tells us to do, and God's order comes to us in the haphazard moments. We do not even make the haphazard moments; God is the arranger of the haphazard. The direction of duty is loyalty to God in our present circumstances.

The Discipline of Distance (22:4)

Though God wants our immediate and constant attention, He is never in a hurry. Abraham had to travel many long hours to the place of sacrifice; this was a journey of isolated reflection for God's servant. And it is evident that Isaac never guessed what was going on between his father and God during that journey—nor did Abraham by word or deed reveal it.

Never reveal to anyone the profound depths of your isolation; when the life of faith is dealing profoundly with God, conceal it. It was this about our Lord that staggered the Pharisees, who wanted everyone to "see" the evidences of their faith. (Piety always pretends to be going through what it is not.) When He might easily have been absorbed in the tremendous moment which He knew was at hand, He revealed no concern for Himself, only for His disciples: "Let not your heart be troubled."

The Devotion of the Devoted (22:5–6)

Abraham held to God's promise (17:19) even as he went to carry out that which would seem to prevent its fulfillment. He did not question God. True faith does not so much take God at His word as it takes the word of God as it is, in the face of all difficulties, and acts upon it, with no attempt to explain or expound it.

The picture in verse 6 is a moving one: Abraham obeying his heavenly Father and Isaac obeying his earthly father. Even when he knew what the purpose was, Abraham was willing to relinquish the joy of his life.

Genesis 22:7–14

The Path of God

"God will provide" (22:8).

The life of Abraham provides a pattern for spiritual biography in which the life ascends from the rational and accountable to the personally traced footsteps of the soul's path to God. The turning points in the spiral ascent of faith are obedience to the effectual call of God and the culmination of unreserved resignation to God.

The Speech of Silent Spirituality (22:7–8)

Abraham and Isaac were spiritually silent: the son was silent before the father, and the father was silent before God; and thus God elevated them both above unspiritual human nature. That is, both father and son went one step beyond the limit of the possible because they were on the path of God. To talk easily about spiritual experiences is an indication that we have only a devout nodding acquaintance with the experiences of others and are devoid of all such experiences ourselves.

In the life of faith the pressure of forethought is transferred to God by the faith which fulfills His behests: we have faith in God's accountable rationality, not in our own. If we have never heard the call of God, all we see is the accountability that we can state to ourselves. Practical work is nearly always a determination to think for ourselves, to take the pressure of forethought on ourselves: I see the need; therefore I must do something. That is not the effectual call of God, but the call of our sympathy with conditions as we see them. When God's call comes, we learn to do actively what He tells us and take no thought for the morrow. Take a step of faith in God, and your rational friends will say: "Very beautiful, but suppose we all did it!" You are not living a life of accountable rationality, but a life of agreement with God's effectual call, and have therefore no reply to make.

In Hebrews 11:17–19 we get further insight into Abraham's spirituality: "By faith Abraham, when he was tested, offered up Isaac . . . of whom it was said, 'In Isaac your seed shall be called,' concluding that God *was* able to raise *him* up, even from the dead." It was not Abraham's common sense but his spiritual illumination that made him know this. However, beware of turning a common-sense somersault and saying that Abraham knew all about it and therefore it was not a sacrifice at all. Abraham did not know all about it; he believed that somehow God would give Isaac back to him. But how? He had no notion. He surrendered himself entirely to the supernatural God.

God never tells us what He is going to do. He simply reveals who He is.

In the obedience of faith Abraham stood in the midst of the most appalling personal controversy, the controversy between natural love and faith, and Isaac was worthy of his father. The path *to* God is never the same as the path *of* God. When we are going on with God in His path, we do not understand, but God does; therefore we understand God, not His path. When we take a step of faith in God and fulfill His behests, God does the forethinking for us. When we do it for ourselves, God has to take second place.

The Sacrifice of Surrendered Sonship (22:9–10)

God is the ruling factor in all our transactions (see Proverbs 20:24). When we commit ourselves to God, He arranges the haphazard, and we have to see that we actively fulfill His behests where He places us.

The binding of Isaac is a prefiguring of the fulfillment and the perfection of the death of Christ. Some today emphasize looking at Christ as our example, rather than as our sacrifice, teaching that it is by prayer and consecration that we come into God's favor. That is absolutely untrue. God never accepts us because we obey; He only accepts us on the ground of sacrifice—the sacrifice of His Son. Personal holiness is never the basis for our acceptance with God; the only ground of acceptance is the death of the Lord Jesus Christ.

The Sympathy of Supreme Spirit (22:11–12)

Abraham had a rational understanding of what God's command meant, but the instant the voice of God came he surrendered himself in devotion to the voice. The essence of true faith is devotion to a Person. Beware of sticking to convictions instead of to Christ; convictions are simply the clothing of your growing life.

Abraham was prepared to do anything for God. Mark the difference between that and doing anything to prove your love to God. Abraham was there to obey God, no matter what that entailed. Abraham was not devoted to his own convictions, or he would have slain his son and said the voice was the voice of the Devil. Faith means giving up your own convictions and traditional beliefs. He did not make declarations, as Peter did, "I will do anything; I will go to death for You." Instead, he remained true to God Himself, and God purified his faith. If we will remain true to God, He will lead us straight through the ordeal into the inner chamber of a better knowledge of Himself.

The sacrifice of death is not the final thing God wants. What God wants is the sacrifice through death which enables a man to do what Jesus did—that is, sacrifice his life (see Romans 12:1). Many of us think that God wants us to give up things; we make Christianity the great apotheosis of giving up! God purified Abraham from this blunder, and the same discipline goes on in our lives. "Oh well, I expect God will ask me to give that up," we say. God nowhere tells us to give up things for the sake of giving them up; He tells us to give them up for the sake of the only thing worth having—life with Himself. It is a question of loosening the bands that hinder our life, and as soon as those bands are loosened by identification with the death of Jesus, we enter into a relationship with God whereby we sacrifice our life to God. To give God my life for death is of no value; what is of value is to let Him have all my powers that have been saved and sanctified, so that as Jesus sacrificed His life for His Father, I can sacrifice my life for Him. "Present your bodies a *living* sacrifice," said Paul.

The Substitution of Sacramental Service
(22:13–14)

Abraham did not receive an overt command to sacrifice the ram; he recognized in the ram a divine suggestion. When people are intimate with one another, they can communicate by the power of suggestion; and when we come into true fellowship with God, we recognize His suggestions.

Abraham offered the ram as a substitute for his son, and the entire system of sacrifice and substitution is prefigured in this sacrifice of the ram. The spiritual sacrifice of Isaac and the physical sacrifice of the ram are made one; the natural and the spiritual are blended. I, a guilty sinner, can never get right with God; it is impossible. I can only be brought into union with God by *identification with* the One who died in my place. No sinner can get right with God on any other ground than the ground that Christ died in his stead.

Genesis 22:15–19

The Eternal Goal

"I will bless you. . . . because you have obeyed My voice" (22:17, 18).

The spirit of obedience gives more joy to God than anything else on earth. Obedience is impossible to us naturally; even when we do obey, we do it with a pout in our moral underlip and with the determination to scale some moral ladder. In the spiritual domain there is no pout on our face because the nature of God has come into us. When the love of God is shed abroad in our hearts by the Holy Ghost (see Romans 5:5), we are possessed by the nature of God—and the great characteristic of our Lord's life was obedience. By our obedience, we show that we love Him. The best measure of a spiritual life is not its ecstasies, but its obedience. "To obey is better than sacrifice."

The Supreme Call of God (22:15)

When God first called to Abraham, there was still a dim gulf between them; God had to call and Abraham to answer (22:1). Now that gulf is bridged. Abraham is so near to God that he does not need to reply; he is in the place of unimpeded listening. It makes us ask, "Is there any impediment between my ears and God's voice?"

The call of God is a call in accordance with the nature of God, not in accordance with my idea of God. At first Abraham did not interpret the call this way because he did not understand the nature of God; he interpreted it according to the Chaldean tradition and took it to mean he was to kill his son. The supreme crisis in Abraham's faith had now been reached; all his imperfect conceptions of God had been left behind, and he now understood God as He is. Abraham was neither an amateur providence nor a moral policeman; he simply believed God.

The Supreme Reality of God (22:16)

Abraham had come to the place where he was in touch with the very nature of God; he understood the reality of God, and God unveiled Himself in a burst of enthusiasm. There is no possibility of questioning when God speaks to His own nature in us; prompt obedience is the only possible response. When Jesus says, "Come unto Me," we simply come; when He says "Trust in God in this matter," we do not *try* to trust; we *do* trust. An alteration has taken place in our disposition which is an evidence that the nature of God is at work in us.

The Supreme Character of God (22:17–18)

The promise of God stands in relation to Abraham's tried and willing obedience. The revelation of God to us is determined by our character, not by God's (see Psalm 18:25–26). If we are mean, that is how God will appear to us.

By the discipline of obedience we come to the place Abraham reached and see God as He is. The promises of God are of no use to us until by obedience we understand the nature of God. We read some things in the Bible 365 times and they mean nothing to us. Then all of a sudden we see what they mean because in some particular we have obeyed God, and instantly His character is revealed. Our "yea" must be born of obedience. When by the obedience of our life we say "Amen—so let it be" to a promise, then that promise is made ours.

The Supreme Reward (22:19)

The more we have to sacrifice for God, the more glorious will be our reward. We have no right to choose our sacrifice, however; God will let us see what our "Isaac" is to be. God is always at work lifting up the natural and making it and the spiritual one. Yet most of us want to cling to the natural when God wants to put a sword through it. If we go through the transfiguration of the natural, we will receive it back on a new plane altogether. God wants to make eternally our own what we only possessed intermittently.

In the beginning we do not train for God, we train for work, for our own aims; but as we go on with God we lose all our own aims and are trained into God's purpose. Unless practical work is appointed by God, it will prove a curse. "At any cost, by any road," means nothing self-chosen. The Bible does not say that God blessed Abraham and took him to heaven, but that He blessed him and kept him on earth. The maturity of character before God is the personal channel through which He can bless others. If it takes all our lifetime before God can put us right, then others are going to be impoverished. We need to rise as early as we can and climb our Mount Moriah, come to the place where God can put an end to the dim gulf between Him and us. Then He will be able to bless us as He did Abraham.

No language can express the ineffable blessedness of the supreme reward that awaits the soul that has taken its supreme climb, proved its supreme love, and entered on its supreme reward. What an imperturbable certainty there is about the man who is in contact with the real God! Thank God, the life of the father of the faithful is but a specimen of the life of every humble believer who obediently follows the discipline of the life of faith. What a depth of transparent rightness there must be about the man who walks before God, and the meaning of the Atonement is to place us there in perfect adjustment to God. "Walk before Me and be perfect," says the Lord. Not faultless, but blameless—undeserving of censure in the eyes of God.

Genesis 22:20–24

Still Human

Now it came to pass after these things . . . (22:20).

What the natural reason would call an anticlimax is the very climax of God's supernatural grace: a man, having gone through the most wonderful experience, emerges and returns to ordinary life. We find it all through the New Testament. The wonder of the Incarnation slips into the life of ordinary childhood; the marvel of the Transfiguration descends to the valley and the demon-possessed boy; and the glory of the Resurrection merges into breakfast on the seashore in the early dawn.

The tendency in early Christian experience is to look for the marvelous. That is the difference between the fanatic and the faithful. We mistake the sense of the heroic for being heroes. It is one thing to go through a crisis grandly; it is quite another to go through every day glorifying God when there is no crisis, no limelight, and no one paying the remotest attention to us. We may not want medieval haloes, but we want someone to notice; we want something that will make people say, "What a wonderful man of prayer he is! What a pious, devoted woman she is!" If we are rightly devoted to Jesus Christ, we have reached the sublime height where all that is noticed is that the power of God comes through all the time—

145

where we can peel potatoes properly or wash heathen children for the glory of God. Remember: anybody can shine in the sunlight or the footlights.

God's Object and Human Nature (22:20)

The history of the life of Abraham does not close abruptly with his greatest act of faith. Instead, there is a natural human progress to a sanctified life. Human nature likes to read about the heroic and the intense: it takes the divine nature to be interested in grass and sparrows and trees, because they are so unutterably commonplace, and also because God happens to have made them.

Any sordid being can sit in a cathedral in the twilight and listen to beautiful music and feel divine; Abraham lived as God's man in the earthly conditions of his ordinary life. If the indwelling of God cannot be manifested in human flesh, then the Incarnation and the Atonement are of no avail. All our Christian work may be merely scaffolding poles to prepare us so that God may do what He likes with us unobtrusively. The test of the life of a saint is not success, but faithfulness as a steward of the mysteries of God in human life as it actually is. The one thing glorifying to God is the glory of God manifested in ordinary human lives. The "show business" belongs to the pagan order; devotion to God in actual human conditions belongs to the redemptive order. A Christian is one who has learned to live the life hid with Christ in God in human conditions.

God's Opportunity and Human Forethought (22:21–23)

The message Abraham received was providential and came at the right moment. It was all in the order of God. Abraham would soon have to think of Isaac's marriage, and the information about his kindred caused him to hope that he might find a bride for Isaac in his brother's family.

Remain true to God in your obscurity, and remember you are not the designer of your destiny. When you hear the call of God and realize what He wants, obey Him, because away in some other part of the world there are other circumstances being worked by God that may depend on your circumstances. Half the sentimental, pious folks that strew the coasts of emotional religious life are there because they would engineer their own circumstances.

God's omniscience, God's order, and God's opportunity all work together in individual lives, and Jesus Christ enters into our lives right in the midst of seemingly haphazard circumstances. Sanctification is not the end of redemption; it is the gateway to the purpose of God. Christian experience is not the purpose of redemption. God's own plans are the purpose of redemption.

Human Greatness

And the sons of Heth answered Abraham, saying to him . . .
"You *are* a mighty prince among us; bury your dead in the
choicest of our burial places" (23:5–6).

The life of faith does not consist solely of acts of worship or
of great self-denial and heroic virtues; the life of faith is all the
daily conscious acts of our lives. The life of faith affects all the
places of our lives.

Abraham kept company with God until he became a par-
taker of the divine nature. It is impossible for a saint, no matter
what his experience, to keep right with God if he will not take
the trouble to spend time with God. In order to keep the mind
and heart awake to God's high ideals we have to keep coming
back again and again to the primal source. Just as a poet or an
artist must keep his soul brooding on the creative, so a Christian must keep his soul awake to the sense of God's call. Let
other things go; spend time with God. We are not here to do
work *for* God, but to be workers *with* Him—those through
whom He can do His work.

In the Place of Sorrow (23:1–2)

The Old Testament relates the end of no other woman's
life as particularly as it does the end of Sarah's life, and Abra-

ham's personal sorrow is recorded in the words, "Abraham came to mourn for Sarah and to weep for her." Faith does not deny death, nor does it suppress the natural expressions of the human heart; faith is not insensible to sorrow. In certain stages of religious experience we have the idea that we must not show sorrow when we are sorrowful. That is stoical humbug, and it leads to heartlessness and hypocrisy. Not to sorrow is not even human; it is diabolical. The Spirit of God hallows sorrow.

In the Place of Sojourning (23:3–4)

The phrase Abraham uses to describe himself, "a stranger and sojourner" (KJV), is the inner meaning of the term "Hebrew." Abraham could never say that he was at home in Canaan; he left his home, never to find another on earth. The Hebrews were deeply conscious of their lot as pilgrims, and we need to take note of this.

Instead of being pilgrims and strangers on the earth, too often Christians entrench themselves as citizens of this world. The genius of the Spirit of God is to make us pilgrims so that there is continual un-at-home-ness in this world (see Philippians 3:20). It is a matter of indifference to the Spirit of God where we are, and we ought to be equally indifferent. As saints, we are cursed, not blessed, by patriotism. The idea of nations is man's, not God's. His kingdom is not built on civilizations. When our Lord establishes His reign there will be no nations, only the great kingdom of God.

In the Place of Sentiment (23:8–9)

Sentiment is thought occasioned by feeling; sentimentality is feeling occasioned by thought. Sentiment plays an important part in human affairs, and no sentiment is more sacred than that connected with our dead. Disaster or bereavement produce emotions that are the bedrock of feeling which makes human life worthy. As Christians we should conduct our lives on the high sentiment that is the outcome of a transaction with the Lord Jesus Christ. If our testimony is weak, it is because we have gone through no crisis with God; there is no heart-broken emotion behind it. If we have been through a crisis in which human feeling has been plowed to its inner center by the Lord, our testimony will convey all the weight of the greatness of God along with human greatness. It is essential to go through a crisis with God which costs you something; otherwise your devotional life is not worth anything. You cannot be profoundly moved by doctrine; you can only be profoundly moved by devotion.

The Hittites had no word for "gentleman," so they called Abraham "a mighty prince." This did not mean that they saw him as some kind of earthly royalty. They were bowing not to any trappings of wealth or station, but to his true greatness of spirit. Most of us only recognize human trappings. We bow to money and birth. If we bow because we must, we are conventional frauds. If we bow because we recognize true greatness, it is a sign we are being emancipated. The greatest humiliation for a Christian is to recognize that he has ignored true greatness because it was without trappings. If the Pharisees had recognized true greatness, they would not have treated the Nazarene carpenter as they did.

Genesis 24

Beatific Betrothal

"Come in, O blessed of the LORD! Why do you stand outside?" (24:31).

Nothing exceeds the dignity and beauty of this chapter which reveals God's providential workings in the lives of several upright people and clearly conveys God's order for each one. In the case of Abraham we see sublime sentiment being worked out in plain common-sense details, yet with the natural sensibilities alive to human conditions and to the demands of God.

As already stated, there is a difference between sentiment and sentimentality. We cannot be profoundly moved by thought; we can only be profoundly moved by a personal crisis with God in which our usual equilibrium is disturbed. If the disturbance comes to us from outside, we will be exactly the same after it; but if we go through a personal crisis such as the personal crisis of devotion to our Lord in discipleship, then all our conceptions of life will take color from that moment.

People who are merely sentimentally pious have had no crisis; all they have is the affectation of sentimentality. Recall the depths of feeling through which God has taken Abraham. Now in this chapter we see him being led rightly in the actual concerns of life. Right views on profound matters will always be the spring of right relationships in more mundane matters. God is the one who welds both faith and common sense into one practical personality.

Any feature of actual life not brought under the severe control of the conception born of your crisis with God will leave a loophole for the Devil. For instance, if you ignore certain aspects of your practical human existence—take too much sleep, or not enough sleep, or forego meals—you will give occasion to the enemy straightaway, no matter how great a saint you are. All this is a matter of "sense" in understanding matters of practical human existence.

The problem with Christians is that we will not learn from the crisis we have had; consequently when we come to the things of sense and meet with people who have not had a crisis with God, it is an easy matter to climb down from God's standard. If we remain true to the sentiment produced in us by our crisis with God, those who protest against us will ulti- mately have to come up to the same standard.

Solemn Sacredness of Serving (24:2–3)

"The oldest servant of [Abraham's] house, who ruled over all that he had" was probably Eliezer of Damascus. Eliezer in many respects is representative of what a disciple of the Lord should be; the whole molding of his life was his devotion to his master, not to a sense of right or duty. We know very little about devotion to Jesus Christ. We know about devotion to right and to duty, but none of that is saintly; it is purely natural. Our sense of duty and right can never be God's. If we can state what our duty is, we have become gods in that particular. There is only One who knows what my duty is as a Christian, and that is God. The Sermon on the Mount no- where tells us what our duty is; it tells us the things a saint will do. Be renewed in the spirit of your mind, says Paul, not that you may do your duty, but that you may make out what God's will is.

All Eliezer seeks is the happiness of his master; self-remembrance in him is dead. He is shrewd and practical, yet as guileless as a child—the exact embodiment of 1 Corinthians 4:2: "Moreover it is required in stewards that one be found faithful."

Self-Forgetfulness in Stewards of Secrets (24:16–17)

One significant thing to notice is that Rebecca came alone and unveiled and conversed freely with a stranger. Eliezer's self-forgetfulness and Rebecca's own intuition made her know that she was safe with him. There are those who talk like angels, yet they smudge the soul; there are others who may not talk sweetly yet they exhilarate the soul. Guard your intuition as the gift of God. You cannot judge virtue by its opposite; you can only judge virtue by intuition. Woe be to anyone who ignores the intuitive warning that says: Now draw back. For God's sake and your own, draw back; it matters not who the person is.

Sweet Supremacy of Singleness (24:50)

Rebecca's brother and mother recognized God's hand in the whole matter, and Rebecca's consent was sought only on the point of departure. When Rebecca said, "I will go," it was an answer to Eliezer's prayer. Rebecca felt the thrill that always passes through any pure young heart in the presence of a saint. A soul's trust in a saint in the providence of God is something more precious even than love. Few of us know anything about it because we are too sordidly selfish; we want things for ourselves all the time. Eliezer had only one loyalty— to his master, and in the providence of God he brought Rebecca straight to Isaac. This marriage, like all true marriages, concerns the kingdom of God.

Genesis 24

Discovering Divine Designs

Then the man bowed down his head and worshiped the
LORD (24:26).

The whole discipline of the life of faith is to make the ideal
visions of faith and the actual performance of life one in personal possession. In art and literature the ideal and the actual
are only made one in a picture or a poem or book. In our
personal life, the ideal and the actual are only made one by the
Holy Spirit. The temple of the Holy Ghost is our personal life.

Human Forethought and Divine Design (24:1–9)

Abraham's motive is clearly stated here. Never speak of
human motives as if they were opposed to the divine. In the
life of a child of God the human motive is the disguised divine.
Sanctification means that I become a child of God; consequently my common-sense decisions are God's will unless He
gives the check of His Spirit. I decide things in perfect fellowship with God, knowing that if my decisions are wrong, He
will check. When He checks, I must stop at once. It is the
inner check of the Spirit that prevents common sense from
being our god.

If God is not recognized by His blessings in the details of
actual life in the beginning, He will be recognized in the end by

His destructions. Human forethought in a faithful soul such as Abraham is the manifestation of the divine design. In looking back you see not the haphazard, but an amazing design which, if you are born of God, you will credit to God; otherwise you credit it to the extraordinary wisdom of men and women.

Human Appointments and Divine Discoveries (24:10–21)

It is our wisdom to follow providence, but folly to force it. By earnest human effort Eliezer makes his appointments, and these are not only recognized by God, but become avenues for discovering the divine mind. Unless you are a saint, your praying is pious humbug; but if you are a saint, you soon realize that you discover the divine by energetically doing the human—provided you are maintaining a personal relationship to God. The fanatical element in the saint is the element that is devoted to a principle instead of to consistent conduct before God. For instance, I may become a devotee of the doctrine of divine healing which means I must never be sick, and if I am sick then I say I must have gone wrong. The battle is against the absurdity of being consistent to an ideal instead of to God.

The vital point about Eliezer is not his asking for signs, but that *Eliezer* asked for signs. Eliezer was a man who related everything entirely to God; consequently his human appointments, which are easy to ridicule, were God's way of enabling him to discover His mind. Beware of making a fetish of consistency to convictions instead of developing your faith in God. Whenever we take what God has done and put it in the place of God Himself, we instantly become idolaters. If our Lord had been fanatically consistent, He would have said after the temptation, "I have not eaten for forty days; therefore I will never eat food again." He did not eat for forty days because it was

His Father's will for Him not to. Judged on the line of logical consistency there was no more inconsistent being than our Lord. He said, "Resist not evil," and then He cleansed the temple in Jerusalem. But our Lord was never inconsistent to His Father. The saint is to be consistent to the divine life within him, not logically consistent to a principle. A fanatic is concerned not about God but about proving his own little fanatical ideas. This is a danger peculiar to us all. It is easier to be a fanatic than a faithful soul because there is something amazingly humbling, particularly to our religious conceit, in being loyal to God.

Human Astonishment and Divine Details
(24:22–33)

The details of these verses are commonplace to Eastern custom, but Eliezer sees God in them. It is easy to see God in exceptional things or in a crisis, but it requires the culture of spiritual discipline to see God in every detail. Never allow that the haphazard is anything less than God's appointed order.

The other thing to note in these verses is the characteristic of the hospitality; it is an incurious, generous hospitality, which is the rarest type. Hospitality is characteristic not only of the East but of God's program.

Human Affinities and Divine Directions
(24:34–49)

Eliezer gives a simple account of his journey, but his speech is an example of great wisdom. When the Spirit of God guides a man's human affairs, his speech indicates not human shrewdness, but the frankness of divine skill. We must be ready to discover divine designs *anywhere*.

Human Abandon and Divine Devotion (24:50–67)

Laban and Bethuel recognized the will of God in this whole matter. When a soul abandons to God, God will not abandon it. But let that soul trust its wits and become its own amateur providence and a dexterous muddle will be the result. Amateur providence prevents your doing the thing God tells you to do: "I must not tell my parents about my call; I want to prevent them from suffering." Your plain duty before God is to tell them. If you are abandoned to God and do the duty that lies nearest, God will not abandon you; but if you trust in your wits, He will have to abandon you, and there will be heart-breaks and distresses that He is not in at all. Present the whole thing where it ought to be presented, in abandonment to God, and He will engineer everything in His own way.

Genesis 25:1–10

Sunset

Then Abraham breathed his last and died in a good old age, an old man and full *of years,* and was gathered to his people. And his sons Isaac and Ishmael buried him (25:8–9).

It is not what a man achieves, but what he believes and strives for that makes him noble and great. Hebrews 11 expresses this in its elevation of the life of faith above the life of human perfection. The first thing faith in God does is to remove all thought of perfection. Some lives may seem humanly perfect and yet not be relevant to God and His purpose. The effect such lives leave is not of a reach that exceeds its grasp, but of a completed little circle of its own. It takes a man completely severed from God to be perfect in that way. There is a difference between a perfect human life lived on earth and a personal life with God lived on earth; the former grasps that for which it reaches, the latter is grasped by that which it never can reach. The former chains us to earth by its very completeness; the latter causes us to fling ourselves unperplexed on God. The difference is not a question of sin, but the paradox of the incomplete perfection of a right relationship to God.

The Region of the Irrelevant (25:1–4)

One of the most striking features in Abraham's life is its irrelevancy. If we take Abraham to be the embodiment of an idea—say, of sanctification—we will have to cut out much that God puts in. The irrelevant things in Abraham's life are evidences of that half-unconscious living that proves his mind was not taken up with himself. The greatest thing in Abraham's life is God, not "Abrahamism." The whole trend of his life is to make us admire God, not Abraham.

The outstanding characteristic in the life of a saint is its irrelevance—an irrelevance amazingly relevant to the purpose of God. If you become a devotee to a principle, you become a religious lunatic; you are no longer loyal to the life of Jesus, but loyal only to the logic of your convictions about Him. A fanatic dismisses all irrelevancy in life. We say that a lunatic is a man who has lost his reason; actually, a lunatic is a man who has lost everything but his reason. A madman's explanation of things is always complete. The main thing is life, not logic. It is the irrelevant running all through life that makes it worthwhile.

One of the dangers of the so-called higher Christian life movements is the idea that God wants to produce specimens to put in His museum. You can often find better specimens in the world than in the church. Think of the men and women you know who have not been through the crisis you have been through, and your human reason tells you they are infinitely better than you are. They are more unselfish, never irritable or upset: and yet they would not dream of saying what you have to say—that you are loyal to Jesus Christ. The irrelevancy of your life and the relevancy of theirs will produce perplexity in your mind until you remember that you are not called to produce one of God's specimens; you are called to live in perfect relationship to God so that the net result of your life is not admiration for you, but a longing after God. Christian perfection is not, and never can be, human perfection. Christian perfection is the perfection of a relationship to God that shows itself in the total irrelevancy of human life.

If you get swept up in matters like personal holiness or divine healing or the second coming and make any of these your end, you are disloyal to Jesus Christ. Supposing the Lord has healed your body and you make divine healing your end; then the focus of your life is no longer for God but for what you are pleased to call the manifestation of God in your life. "It can never be God's will that I should be sick." Bother your life! If it was God's will to bruise His own Son, why should it not be His will to bruise you? The Christian life is not relevant consistency to an idea of what a saint's life is, but abject abandonment to Jesus Christ whether you are well or ill.

Much of our life is irrelevant to any and every mind saving God's mind. When you obey the call of God, the first thing that strikes you is the irrelevancy of the things you have to do. The idea of human perfection does not leave you with the "flavor" of God at all; it leaves you with the idea that God is totally unnecessary—if by human effort and human devotion we can reach the standard God wants. Well, in a fallen world it cannot be done. Paul refers to this in 2 Corinthians 4:3–4: "whose minds the god of this age has blinded, who do not believe"; that is, they have the perfection of the human, but never once have they seen the perfection of God.

Beware of taking your conception of a saint from deductions from certain Scriptures, and always clarify your views by meditation on John 17. God wants to do with the saints what His Son prayed He would do—make them one with Himself.

The Reign of the Irrevocable (25:5–7)

Ishmael was the son born of the wrong way of doing God's will. If we try to do God's will through our own effort, we produce Ishmael. Much of our modern Christian enterprise is "Ishmael," born not of God, but of an inordinate desire to do God's will in our own way—the one thing our Lord never did.

Ishmael, as we have seen, had to be dismissed and disciplined until he was willing to become subservient and to be used for God's purposes. The natural has to be dismissed and denied until it is willing to be subjected to God, not to our ideas of relevancy. We put sin in the wrong place. Remember, we cannot touch sin. The atonement of the Lord alone touches sin. We must not tamper with it for one second. We can do nothing with sin; we must leave God's redemption to deal with it. Our part has to do with Ishmael, that is, the natural. The natural has to be denied, not because it is bad and wrong, but because it has nothing to do with our life of faith in God until it is turned into the spiritual by obedience. This is the attitude of the maimed life, which so few of us understand.

The Realm of the Irreproachable (25:8)

The Hebrews regarded life as complete when it was full of days and riches and honor. Age was looked upon as a sign of favor. Whenever a nation becomes unspiritual, it reverses this order: the demand is not for old age but for youth. This reversal in modern life is indicative of apostasy, not of advance.

Abraham's life wore to a tranquil sunset. He is described as "full of years"—that is, satisfied with life. He had seen, felt, believed, loved, suffered enough; earth had no more to offer him. Through God's goodness he found goodness in everything. Bitterness and cynicism are born of broken gods; they are an indication that somewhere in my life I have belittled the true God and made a god of human perfection.

The Reunion of the Irreconcilable (25:9–10)

Ishmael and Isaac are reunited at the grave of their father. Strong, rugged Ishmael, representing human perfection; meditative Isaac, incomplete visionary, but on the trail of God. These two unite at the burial of Abraham, the friend of God whom God will not forsake.

Genesis 26:1–12

Abiding Factors

There was a famine in the land, besides the first famine that was in the days of Abraham (26:1).

Isaac's history commences with the same trial as Abraham's, a famine in the land. In fleeing the land, Abraham had acted according to his own wits, not according to his faith in God—destitution in the very land of promise.

Commencement of Destitution (26:1)

Watch the destitution of wits that follows quickly on the heels of a divine revelation. Whenever you get a revelation from God, you will be starved at once—starved, that is, in your wits. You can see no way out. Every time your wits compete with the worship of God you had better take a strong dose of Isaiah 30:15: "In returning and rest you shall be saved; in quietness and confidence shall be your strength." Beware of restlessness and wits persuading you that God has made a blunder: "God would never allow me to fall sick after giving me such a blessing." But He has!

No matter what revelations God has made to you, there will be destitution so far as the physical apprehension of things is concerned. God gives you a revelation that He will provide; then He provides nothing, and you begin to realize that there is a famine—of food, or of clothes, or money—and your common sense says, "Abandon your faith in God." Do it at your peril. Watch where destitution comes. If it comes on the heels of a time of quiet confidence in God, then thank Him for it and hold fast, and He will bring a glorious issue.

Command in Trial (26:2)

The command to Abraham was to depart (12:1); the command to Isaac is to remain. When the Isaac life of quietness and confidence in God is born of the Abraham life of strenuous separation, don't make any more separations; just be still, and know that God is God. Those who educate you in the things of God are often the first to pull you back when you obey the right thing. Now that you are obeying, they come in with their own wits and say, "Of course we didn't mean you should do that." But God did. Beware of mixing quietness and confidence with other people's wits.

Confirmation of Truth (26:3–5)

Isaac is promised divine blessing and protection because of the oath God swore to Abraham. Abraham's obedience was far from perfect, but its great characteristic was its unreservedness. Abandon in the profound sense is of infinitely more value than personal holiness. Personal holiness brings attention to my own whiteness: I dare not be indiscreet, or unreserved; I dare not do anything in case I incur a speck. The holiness produced through the indwelling of God's Son in me is a holiness that is never conscious of itself. There are some people in whom you cannot find a speck, and yet they are not abundantly blessed of God, while others make grave indiscretions and get marvelously blessed. The former have become devotees of personal holiness, conscientious to a degree; the latter are marked by abandonment to God. Whatever centers attention on anything other than our Lord Himself will always lead astray. The only way to be kept cleansed is by walking in the light, as God is in the light. Only as we walk in that light is the holiness of Jesus Christ not only imputed, but imparted, to us.

Abraham's aberrations sprang not from disobedience, but from trusting in his own wits. As soon as God's command was made known to him, he obeyed; when there was no command, however, he was inclined to trust his wits, and that is where he went wrong. It is never right to do wrong in order that right may come. In the long run we can never produce right by doing wrong, yet we will always try to do it unless we believe what the Bible says. If I tell a lie in order to bring about the right, I prove that I do not believe the One at the back of the universe is truthful. Judge everything in the light of Jesus Christ, who is the Truth, and you will never do the wrong thing, however right it looks.

Genesis 26:13–25

The Tender Grace

The man began to prosper, and continued prospering until he became very prosperous (26:13).

The only right a Christian has is the right to give up his rights. This is the tender grace that is usually looked upon as an exhibition of lack of gumption. The embarrassing thing about Christian graces is that as soon as you imitate them, they become nauseating. Conscious imitation implies an affected preference for certain qualities, and we produce frauds by such spurious piety. All the qualities of a godly life are characteristic of the life of God; you cannot imitate the life of God unless you have it. Then the imitation is not conscious, but the unconscious manifestation of the real thing. "Pi" people try to produce the life of God by sheer imitation; they pretend to be sweet when really they are bitter. The life of God is a life without pretence. When His life is in you, you do not pretend to feel sweet; you are sweet.

The External Greatness of Isaac (26:13)

Isaac never became great in the way that Abraham did; his greatness was of a different order. Abraham was not only a great man of God, he was a great *man*. Some lives exhibit grand characteristics, yet have curious defects; the only stan dard for judging the saint is Jesus Christ, not saintly qualities. Beware of the snare of taking people as types; no one is a type of anything. He may recall a particular type, but he is always something other than the type. If Abraham is taken as the type of a saint, he brings embarrassment because of the things in him which were not saintly. We are always inclined to remain true to our own ideas of a person. It does not matter what the facts are; we interpret all that he does according to our idea of him. If I accept you as an expression of my idea of you, I will be unjust to you as a fact. I make you either better or worse than you are. I never hit just "you" until I learn to accept facts as facts.

The Extraordinary Gentleness of Isaac (26:14–25)

Strife arose around wells of living water, and Isaac refused to drink of the water of contention. Whenever a doctrinal well becomes "Esek," give it up; your life with God is more precious than proving you are right doctrinally. It is at the peril of your communion with God that you contend about a doctrine. It is a great sign of grace not to break your heart because you cannot drink of the water of enmity.

Inoffensiveness, which is one of the chief characteristics of Isaac, usually means to our natural minds a quality unsuited to a strong personality. We have to bear in mind that the life of our Lord portrayed just this characteristic; time and again He is described as meek—like a lamb being led to slaughter without a sound. Anything to do with meekness and submissiveness is antagonistic to our view of robust human nature. The natural heart builds on adventure, recklessness, independence, impulse; the characteristics God prizes are produced only in the Son of sacrifice. Natural inoffensiveness may be the weakness of constitutional timidity; supernatural inoffensiveness is almighty strength scorning to use the weapons of the flesh. Inoffensiveness is self-control indwelt by the Holy Ghost.

Following Isaac's refusal to be contentious, God appears to him, and here for the first time we encounter the grand phrase, "I *am* the God of Abraham." And at that point Isaac follows in the footsteps of faith and builds an altar to the Lord.

The Eternal and the Haphazard (26:26–33)

All the transactions entered into by both Abraham and Isaac, no matter how temporary or casual, were based on their relationship to God; that is, they used their wits in their worship of Him. This recognition of God began to be lost during Jacob's life, and the children of Israel went on ignoring it until they came to establish all their transactions on their own wits.

In the Old Testament and in the New Testament record of the Resurrection we find the temporary matters of eating and drinking put on the eternal foundation of relationship to God. The things most easily ridiculed are the things that have most of God in them. A saint can be ridiculed because he sees haphazard happenings in the light of the eternal: "The Lord guided me here, and there." Remember, whatever happens, God is there. It is easy to fix your mind on God in a lecture, but a different matter to fix your mind on Him when there is a war on. You never get at God by blinding yourself to the facts, but only by naming Him in the facts. Say, "Lord, I thank Thee that Thou art here."

Genesis 27

Plans and Providence

Now Rebekah was listening when Isaac spoke to Esau his son (27:5).

Plans arise from the human "must"—the imperative demand of our own undisciplined nature which makes us feel, "I must do something; God is no use here." God rarely rebukes us for our impulsive plans because those plans work their own distress. Plans made apart from trusting God's wisdom are rotten. Providence arises from God's majesty. The wisdom of God can never be according to man's understanding, and in our regenerated lives He engineers our circumstances by His providence and puts within our inmost soul the childlike joy of confidence in Himself. It is always easier not to trust. If we can work the thing out for ourselves, we are not going to trust in God. We work out a plan and thereby try to force God's hand; and when He does what we said we knew He would do, for an exhilarating moment we think we have made Him do it! Then we find we are to be punished for everything we tried to make Him do, though it looks as if our wrong had brought about His good.

Always beware when you can reasonably account to yourself for the action you are about to take, because the source of such clear reasoning is the enthroning of human understanding. It is this element in the personal life of a Christian that fights longest and to the last against the enthronement of Jesus Christ as Lord and Master. "Suppose I do say I will go to the foreign field? What about this and that? I want a reasonable explanation." As long as you argue like that, it is all up with devotion to Jesus Christ. He will have no influence over you because you have put your own wits on the throne. The reason we know so little about God's wisdom is that we will only trust Him as far as we can work things out according to our own reasonable common sense.

Sensitiveness to Divinely Shaped Ends (27:6–17)

Still waters run deep, but an able woman is deeper. Abraham made the supreme blunder of trying to help God fulfill His promise; and Rebekah repeats the blunder. Rebekah carried out her deception as though she was called and inspired of God to do it. In such a case the sin is not the outcome of impulse, but the deliberate perversion of integrity.

When we sin, we always try to blame everything and everybody but ourselves: "My father is to blame . . . my mother . . . my heredity." It is impossible for human wisdom to apportion the blame. There is always the one more fact that God alone knows.

Schemes of Discreet Expectations (27:15–46)

Rebekah enacts a pious lie. Her motive was born of the oracles of God: "and the older shall serve the younger" (25:23), but her act was entirely wrong. She enacted a lie in order to help God carry out His purpose. This is very different from the lie told for our own ends.

Jacob's subsequent enunciation of the lie is expressive fundamentally of devotion to his mother rather than his own self-seeking. Beware of obeying anyone else's obedience to God.

When you do, you are shirking your own responsibility to Him.

When Isaac unwittingly gives Jacob his blessing, the whole lie is now enacted, and Jacob enters into the fullness of the blessing. God foreordained that the blessing should come to Jacob, but it was not part of that foreordination that Jacob should enter into the blessing in the way he did. There are experiences in human lives that are not part of God's purpose, but the result of human perversity. Remember, trust in God does not mean that God will explain His solutions to us; it means that we are perfectly confident in God, and when we do see the solution we find it to be in accordance with all that Jesus Christ revealed of His character. It is nonsense to imagine that God expects me to discern all that is clear to His own mind; all He asks of me is to maintain perfect confidence in Him. Faith springs from the indwelling of the life of God in me.

The Lone Quest

"May God Almighty bless you . . . that you may inherit the land in which you are a stranger, which God gave to Abraham" (28:3, 4).

Jacob's destiny had nothing to do with his personal character, but his personal character had everything to do with the desperate discipline he went through. God's destiny for a life will be fulfilled, though the details of the fulfillment are determined by the individual. The kind of discipline Jacob went through was determined by his perversity. The "lone quest" is never pathetic unless, as in Jacob's case, it is mixed with cunning and sinful motive.

The Discipline of the Unchanging Destiny (28:1–9)

Our natural inclination is to love Esau and dislike Jacob. The most undesirable person in later life is often the one who was most desirable when young. God loves the man who needs Him, and Jacob needed Him. Esau was satisfied with what he was; Jacob wanted to be more than he was. Esau never saw visions, never wrestled with angels, although God was as near to him as to Jacob. Esau refused to sacrifice anything to the spiritual; he could never think of anything but the present. He was willing to sell the promise of the future for a mess of pottage, and thereby he wronged himself far more than Jacob did.

The Dream of the Unimagined Dignity (28:10–22)

Jacob's dream was a vision of the purpose of God for all the families of the earth. The destiny of the people known as Israel is forecast in this one lonely man. God did not *select* this people; He *elected* them. God created them from Abraham to be His servants until through them every nation came to know who Jehovah was. They mistook the election of God's purpose to be the election of God's favoritism, however, and the story of their distress is due to their determination to use themselves for purposes other than God's. To this day they survive miraculously so that the purpose of God may be fulfilled through them. They can still wait, still see visions of God, and the time is coming when God's promise shall be fulfilled materialistically. The prophecies are frequently taken as pictures of spiritual blessings; they are much more than that.

Jacob's ladder symbolizes communication between God and man. The only Being in whom communication with God was never broken was the Lord Jesus Christ, and His claim is that through redemption He can put every one of us in the place where communication with God can be re-established. Paul's phrase "in Christ"—the mystical Christ, not the historic Christ—is a revelation of redemption at work on our behalf. If I am "in Christ," the angels of God are always ascending and descending on my behalf, and the voice that speaks is the voice of God (see John 1:51).

Beware of having a measuring rod for the Almighty, of tying God up in His own laws. This pre-incarnate vision of God was given to Jacob just as he was, not because of some merit of his own. As soon as prayer or devotion are taken as the ground of God's blessing, we are off the track. Prayer and devotion are simply the evidence that we are on God's plan; to be devoid of any sense of ill-being spiritually is a sign that we are not on God's plan. Jacob is the man who represents life as it is. The world is not made up of saints or of devils, but of people like you and me, and our real home is at the foot of the ladder with Jacob—in the desolate place. Jesus Christ makes the real and the actual one, as they were in His own life. We cling to the certainty that the rational, common-sense life is the right one; Jesus Christ stands for the fact that a life based on the Redemption is the only right one. Consequently when a man shifts from the one to the other, there is a period of desolation. Remember, there is a vast moral distance between Bethel and Peniel.

The Dedication of the Unparalleled Dawn
(28:16–22)

It is in the dark night of the soul that the realization of God's presence breaks upon us. We never see God as long as, like Esau, we are perfectly satisfied with what we are. When we are certain that "in me dwelleth no good thing," we begin to experience the miracle of seeing and hearing, not according to our senses, but according to the way the Holy Spirit interprets the word of God to us. When the revelation of God's presence does come, it comes to those who are where Jacob was—in downright need and depression, with no vestige of human sufficiency—knowing there is no help anywhere saving in God. There, in "that place," where it is not within the bounds of human imagination to believe that God could be, He comes to us. And there is always an amazed surprise when we find what God brings with Him when He comes, for He brings everything!

When we come to consider it, the phrase "the God of Jacob" is the greatest possible inspiration, for it contains the whole meaning of the Gospel of Jesus Christ, who said, "I come not to call the righteous, but sinners." Had we been left with "the God of Joseph" or "the God of Daniel," it could have left us with a sense of hopeless despair. But "the God of Jacob" means "God is my God," the God not only of the noble character, but of the sneak. From the sneak to entire sanctification is the miracle of the grace of God.

Genesis 29

Love

Now Jacob loved Rachel (29:18).

Love, more than any other experience in life, reveals the shallowness and the profundity, the hypocrisy and the nobility, of human nature. In dealing with something as implicit as love, there is a danger of being sentimentally consistent to a doctrine or an idea while actual life is ignored; we forget that we have to live in this world as human beings. Consistency in doctrine ought to work out into expression in actual life; otherwise we have only a shadow of the real thing. Anything that makes a man keep up a posture is not real. For example, it is not true to say that an understanding of the doctrine of sanctification will lead you into the experience. Doctrinal exposition comes after the experience in order to bring the actual life into perfect harmony with the marvel of the work of God's grace.

God and the Cult of the Passing Moment (29:1–7)

The true worship of God can only be maintained when the passing moments are seen as occurring in God's order. If you try to forecast the way God will work, you will get into a muddle. Live the life of a child and you will find that every haphazard occasion fits into God's order. "The cult of the passing moment" means that you resolutely believe that "all things work together for good to them that love God, to them who are the called according to His purpose." Don't be your own god in these matters; be concentrated not on the haphazard, but on God, who comes to you through the haphazard.

Jacob realized God's order in the midst of the haphazard circumstances in which he found himself. In the coming of Rachel he suddenly met God.

God and the Cult of the Passionate Moment (29:8–14)

There is no safer guide in the matter of human love than the Bible, particularly the Old Testament. Solomon says a penetrating thing: "Do not stir up nor awaken love until it please"—before the time (Song of Solomon 2:7). Many a man has awakened love before the time and has reaped hell into the bargain. Love is awakened before the time whenever a man or woman ignores the worship of God and becomes a mere creature of impulsive passions. God cannot guard the natural heart that does not worship Him; it is at the mercy of every vagrant passion stirred by the nearness of another.

Beware of not worshiping God in your emotional life. Watch your fancies and your friends, heed who you love and who loves you, and you will be saved from many a pitfall.

God and the Cult of the Parenthetic Moment (29:15–20)

Jacob was what he was—mean. Yet in the meanest human life there may come a parenthesis that is pure and unsullied. Mark well the parentheses God puts into your life. There is not a passage in the whole of the Bible to equal verse 20 for a description of pure human love: "So Jacob served seven years for Rachel, and they seemed *only* a few days to him because of the love he had for her." Sacrifice for love is never conscious;

sacrifice for duty always has margins of distress. The nature of love is to give, not to receive. Talk to a lover about giving up anything, and he doesn't begin to understand you!

Love is not blind. Love sees a great deal more than the actual; it sees the ideal in the actual, and consequently the actual is transfigured by the ideal. That is something quite different from "halo-slinging," which means you have your own idea about other people and expect them to live up to it, and then when they don't you blame them. An ideal is not a halo, it is reality made clear to you by intuition. If you love someone, you are not blind to his defects, but you see that ideal which exactly fits that one. God sees all our crudities and defects, but He also sees the ideal for us; He sees "every man perfect in Christ Jesus." Consequently He is infinitely patient.

God and the Cult of the Paralleled Measure
(29:25–35)

The humor of God is sometimes tragic, for He engineers across our path the kind of people who exhibit to us our own characteristics. Not very flattering, is it? In this chapter we see the beguiler beguiled. Jacob was deceived, but he also was a deceiver. We say, "I wonder why this should happen to me." Remember the apostle Paul's words: "He who does wrong will be repaid for what he has done, and there is no partiality" (Colossians 3:25).

Genesis 30

Degeneration

Now when Rachel saw that she bore Jacob no children,
Rachel envied her sister (30:1).

Degeneration and backsliding are by no means one and the
same. Degeneration begins in almost imperceptible ways; backsliding in the scriptural use of the term is a distinct forsaking of
what we know of God and a deliberate substitution of something other (see Jeremiah 2:13).

A point on which we need to be alert is that the presence
of the life of the Son of God in us does not alter our human
nature; God does remove the disposition of sin, but He demands that our human nature "puts on the new man" so that it
no longer fashions itself according to its former natural desires.
This is what the apostle Paul means by "put to death" in
Colossians 3:5—that is, destroy by neglect. The spiritual application is that the natural must be sacrificed in order that it may
be turned into the spiritual.

Esau stands for the natural life refusing to obey. If I maintain my right to my natural self, I will begin to degenerate and
get out of God's purpose. What happens in my personal life
when I am born from above is that the Son of God is born in
me. Then comes in this law of the sacrifice of the natural to the
spiritual, and the possibility of degeneration. If I refuse to
sacrifice the natural, the God-life in me is killed.

When the Reward of Sin Is More Sinfulness

Jacob received retribution for his own deceitfulness. He impersonated Esau; Laban made Leah impersonate Rachel. Beware what you permit in your relationships because you will "be-done-by-as-you-did," and the reason for it is God. The inexorable law is stated in Matthew 7:2: "For with what judgment you judge, you will be judged; and with the measure you use, it will be measured back to you." The wrong began with Abraham and Hagar, and it works straight through the family; the only extrication is through redemption.

Where the Ruin of Sanctity Is Mixed Sanctity (30:1–24)

Jacob's home becomes a place of friction—no man ever gave his heart to two women—yet gleams of joy come to it. Every child is regarded by the Hebrew as a gift of God, and the naming of Jacob's children reveals this.

If you indulge in practices or imaginations that the Holy Spirit condemns, the appalling lash of ruined sanctity is that "your sin will find you out." God has made the way of transgressors hell on earth. The first mark of degeneration is to deem a wrong state permissible and then propose it as a condition of sanctity. We only turn in disgust from the details in God's Book when we forget who we are. Nothing has ever been done by human nature that any member of the human family may not be trapped into doing. The only safeguard is to keep in the light as God is in the light.

Where Retribution of Selfishness Turns to Spite (30:25–43)

Jacob has been robbed, and now he retaliates. His aim is to enrich himself at Laban's expense, and he succeeds absolutely.

Beware of the inspiration that springs from impulse, because impulse enthrones self-lordship as God. My impulses can never be disciplined by anyone save myself—not even by God. Unless I discipline my impulses, they will ruin me, no matter how generous they may be. The revelation to ourselves in studying other people's lives—like the lives in this chapter—ought to make us eager to realize that "in me dwelleth no good thing."

Genesis 31

The Crisis in Circumstances

Then the LORD said to Jacob, "Return to the land of your fathers" (31:3).

No man's destiny is made for him; each man makes his own. Fatalism is the deification of moral cowardice that arises from a refusal to accept the responsibility for choosing either of the two destined ends for the human race: salvation or damnation. The power of individual choice is the secret of human responsibility. I can choose which line I will go on, but I have no power to alter the destination of that line once I have taken it; yet I always have the power to get off one line and on to the other.

Confusion in Consecration (31:1–10)

Jacob seems to think that to do things openly when you might do them obscurely is a sign of feeble intelligence; all his outwitting has not taught him wisdom. The apparent piece of humbug which these verses record is not really humbug at all; it is a repetition of what happened in the matter of the birthright, in which Isaac and Rebekah, Jacob and Esau, all did wrong, and yet out of it came the fulfillment of God's purpose. The blunder lies in trying to help God fulfill His own word. God's word will be fulfilled, but if I reach its fulfillment through committing sin, God must crush me in chastisement. The chastisement has no part in His order; it comes in under His permissive will.

Call to Conscience (31:11–13)

Jacob is reminded of his dream at Bethel when God appeared to him and spoke to him. Jacob's character exhibits human nature better than any other Bible character—the high mountain peaks and the cesspools, they all come out. No man is so bad but that he is good enough to know he is bad.

Beware of insisting on attainments that are impossible to human nature before the possibilities of the divine nature have come in—demanding of human nature that it should be what it never can be. Jesus Christ died for the *ungodly,* for the *weak,* for *sinners;* if we put the fruits of the Redemption as the reason for God's forgiveness, we belittle His salvation. God's call comes not to human nature, but to conscience, and when a man obeys what God reveals to a thoroughly awakened conscience, then begins the possibility in human nature of the expression of the life of God. To experience conviction of sin is not a cause for misgiving, but an occasion for understanding the impossible thing God has done in the Redemption.

Calamity in Estrangement (31:14–35)

Jacob's flight—and its attendant perplexities—is the best unveiling of the unutterable muddle the most acute human wisdom can get into, and serves as another indication of the truth of the revelation that "A man's goings are of the Lord; how then can man understand his way?" Crises reveal that we don't believe this; the only God we worship is our own wits. A personal crisis ought to serve as an occasion for revealing the fact that God reigns, as well as compelling us to know our own character. You may think yourself to be generous and noble until a crisis comes, and you suddenly find you are a cad and a coward; no one else finds it out, but you do. To be found out by yourself is a terrible thing.

Rachel outwits Laban and Jacob by stealing the household gods, which were like a talisman or a mascot supposed to bring good luck. A reawakening of superstition always follows on the heels of gross materialism in personal and in national life. When once the mascot tendency is allowed in the temple of the Holy Ghost, spiritual muddle-headedness is sure to result. Beware of excusing spiritual muddle-headedness in yourself; if it is not produced by the Jacob reserve, it is produced by the Rachel wit, and the only way out of the muddle is to walk in the light.

Genesis 32

Mahanaim

When Jacob saw [the angels of God], he said, "This *is* God's camp" (32:2).

Of all the Bible characters, Jacob remains the best example of the recipient of God's life and power simply because of the appalling mixture of the good and the bad, the noble and the ignoble in him. We have the notion that it is only when we are pure and holy that God will appear to us; that God's blessing is a sign that we are right with Him. Neither notion is true. Our Lord took care to tell us that He makes the sun rise on the evil as well as the good and sends His rain on the just as well as the unjust. God's blessings are not to be taken as an indication of the integrity of the character who is blessed; yet on the other hand, the discernment of God's character is determined entirely by the individual character of the person estimating God. "With the merciful You will show Yourself merciful" (see Psalm 18:24–26). The way we discern God's character is determined by our own character. God remains true to His character, and as we grow in integrity we discern Him. Jacob's undeservedness and the fact that God continually blessed him are brought out very clearly all through his life.

The Venture of the Misgiving Way

A sense of personal unworthiness is frequently the reaction of overweening conceit; genuine unworthiness has no conscious interest in itself. A genuinely unworthy nature is always possessed of sufficient nobility to face the inevitable. The study of Jacob under the light of the Spirit of God is not exhilarating, but it is a wholesome cure for spiritual swagger. Whenever you get a real dose of your own unworthiness, you are never conscious of it because you are so certain you are unworthy that you have the courage of despair. The first thing the Spirit of God does when He comes in is to bring this sense of unworthiness. Most of us suspend judgment about ourselves; we find reasons for not accusing ourselves entirely. Consequently the definiteness and intensity of the Bible revelation prompts us to say it exaggerates, until we are smitten with the knowledge of what we are like in God's sight.

If you can come to God without a sense of your own contemptibility, it is questionable whether you have ever come. The most humiliating thing in self-examination is that the passion of indignation we indulge in regarding others is the measure of our self-detection (see Romans 2:1).

The Vision of the Ministering Witnesses (32:1)

The appearances of God are not so much a testimony to the goodness of the individual as the revelation of God Himself. Every estimate of God must be brought to the standard of the revelation made of Him by our Lord. The appearance of the angels of God is apt to be looked upon as the result of disordered nerves. It is only when external conditions are hopeless to the human outlook that we are in a fit state to perceive the revelation. We are content where we are as long as things have not got to the hopeless condition, and when we do get there we are sentimentally interested in our own pathos: "Whatever shall I do when this or that happens?" When it does, you will see the angels of God.

There is no such thing as dull despair anywhere in the Bible. There is tragedy of the most appalling order, but an equally amazing hopefulness—always a door deeper down than hell which opens into heaven.

The Voice of the Mastering Wonder (32:2)

The sight of the two hosts, the earthly and the heavenly, is a fitting revelation of God's rule and government in this order of things. So few of us see the hosts of God because we have never let go of things as they are, never let go of our small parochial notions, of the sense of our own whiteness and respectability; consequently there is no room for God at all. Beware of the abortion of God's grace which prostitutes the Holy Spirit to the personal, private use of our own whiteness, instead of allowing God by His majestic grace to keep us loyal to His character in spite of everything that transpires. Faith in God does not mean that He presents us as museum specimens, but it does mean that however ignoble we may feel, we remain true to God's character no matter what perplexities may rage.

God's angelic hosts are like His visible mercies—countless. We are economically drunk nowadays. Everybody is an economist; consequently we imagine that God is economical. Think of God in creation! Think of the number of trees and the blades of grass and flowers, the extravagant wealth of beauty no one ever sees! Think of the sunrises and sunsets we never look at! God is lavish in every degree. For God's sake, don't be economical!

Genesis 32:3–21

Misgiving

So Jacob was greatly afraid and distressed (32:7).

Misgiving is, in a word, the pathetic poem of the whole of human life. It signifies the destruction of confidence. Many things will destroy confidence. As in the case of Jacob, cunning and sin will do it, or cowardice; but in every experience of misgiving there is an element that is difficult to define, and the shallow element is the most difficult. "I can't understand why I have no confidence in God," we say. It may be a matter of digestion, not enough fresh air or sleep, or too much tea—something that slight. It is the shallow things that put us wrong much more quickly than the big things. The great object of the enemy of our souls is to make us fling away our confidence in God; to do this is nothing less than spiritual suicide. When we experience misgiving because we have sinned, there is never any ambiguity as to its cause. The Holy Spirit brings conviction home like a lightning flash.

The Appointment of the Messengers
(32:3–5)

Jacob has had a vision of God's power, but now he begins to put prudent methods on foot in case God should be obliged to let him down on account of his cunning. We have all got a

Uriah Heep tucked away somewhere inside us, and his original is found in Jacob. Every one of us is capable of every type of meanness humanity has ever exhibited; not to believe this is to live in a fool's paradise.

The Apprehension of the Maneuvers
(32:6–8)

Jacob has no intention of confessing his wrong, and his apprehensiveness on this account leads him to maneuver. Beware of the "yes-but"; of putting your prudence-crutch under the purpose of God when you find His engineering of things has nearly unearthed your own little bag of tricks. Whenever you debate with a promise of God, watch how you begin to maneuver by your own prudence—but you can't sleep at night. Whenever you maneuver, it keeps up a ferment because it indicates a determination not to confess where you know you are wrong. And when we experience misgiving on account of wrongdoing we do not intend to confess, we are always inclined to put a crutch under God's promise: "Now I see how I can make atonement for my wrongdoing." Nothing can atone for wrong except an absolutely clean confession to God. To walk in the light with nothing folded up is our conscientious part. God will do the rest.

The Appeal of Misgiving (32:9–12)

Prayer in distress dredges the soul. It is a good thing to keep a note of the things you pray about when you are in distress. We remain ignorant of ourselves because we do not keep a spiritual autobiography. Jacob's misgivings while in the attitude of prayer arise from the fact that while there is that in him which causes him to obey God, he is apprehensive lest God should punish him for his wrongdoing. He has to come to the place where he willingly confesses his guilt before

God. Remember, Jacob did not turn back; he was cunning and crafty, but he was not a coward. There was not a strand of the physical coward in Jacob, but he was a moral coward by reason of his guilty conscience. His misgivings arose from his misdeeds.

Beware of having plans in your petitions before God; they are the most fruitful source of misgiving. If you pray along the line of your plans, misgivings are sure to come; and if the misgivings are not heeded, you will pervert God's purpose in the very thing that was begun at His bidding. God begins a work by the inspiration of the Holy Spirit for His own ends entirely. Then we get caught up into His purpose for that thing, and we begin to introduce our own plans. We storm the throne of God along that line. And the first thing God does is not to do it, and we say, "That must be the devil." Beware of making God an item, even the principal item, in your program. God's ways are curiously abrupt with programs; He seems to delight in breaking them up.

The Atonement for Misdeeds (32:13–21)

Watch your motive for giving presents; it is a good way of discerning what a mean sneak you are capable of being. The giving of presents is one of the touchstones of character. If your relationship with God is not right in your present-giving, you will find there is an abomination of self-interest in it some-where, even though you do it out of a warm-hearted impulse; there is a serpent-insinuation in it. It creeps into all your charity unless your life is right with God.

The cunning way in which the present is made to Esau is obvious, and yet Jacob is getting near the place where "Peniel" is possible. Restitution in some form or other is as certain as the fact that God is on His throne. Watch the uncanny accuracy with which the Holy Spirit will bring a thing back. Beware how you deal with yourself when God is educating you down to the scruple. Human nature looks for something big; yet it is nearly always some ridiculously small thing that keeps you from getting through to God, for behind it is the disposition of your prideful right to yourself.

Genesis 32:22–32

Peniel

So Jacob called the name of the place Peniel (32:30).

Peniel means "face of God," and it recalls the words that will come to Moses generations later: "You cannot see My face; for no man shall see Me, and live" (Exodus 33:20). These words give peculiar force to Jacob's words, "I have seen God face to face, and my life is preserved," for Jacob did see God face to face, and he did die—so profound a death that God gave him a new name. "Your name shall no longer be called Jacob, but Israel."

That is always the test of the reality of sanctification: not so much that I have received something, but that I have ceased to be my old self. Through disillusionment and shattering Jacob comes out on God's side with a changed name; we drag the purpose of God through our own plans and change His name. We have to learn to distinguish between the impression made on us by a vision and identification with the One who gave us the vision. The love of God and His forgiveness are the first things we experience; we are not prepared as yet to recognize His other attributes of holiness and justice because that will mean death to everything that does not partake of God's nature.

The Struggle of Anguish (32:22–25)

In his loneliness Jacob goes through the decisive struggle of his life. We are dealing in this chapter with Jacob the giant, not with Jacob the mean man. Jacob tried to strangle the answer to his own prayer; his wrestling represents the human fighting with God. The nobler ones in God's sight are those who do not struggle but go through without demur. Abraham did not wrestle; neither did Isaac. Jacob struggles for everything.

If a man has difficulty in getting through to God, we are apt to imagine it is an indication of a fine character, whereas the opposite is true. He is refusing to yield and is kicking, and the only thing God can do is to cripple him. The characteristics exhibited by Jacob are those of Peter before Pentecost, of Saul before the Damascus road: a mixture of the dastardly and the heroic, the mean and the noble, all jumbled up. There is not one word about Esau in all that follows, for Jacob's wrestling is a profounder thing than the meeting with his brother. Jacob is face to face with his need to acknowledge God and be blessed by Him.

The Surrender of All (32:26)

When the supreme crisis is reached in a mixed soul like Jacob, something must die—either self-realization or God. To the simpler nature the crisis need not come at all, but to the mean, the ambitious, and the proud it must come, and God does not show Himself as gentle, but as adamant. What is put to death depends on us. Are we willing to let the wrong that cannot dwell with God die, or to let the life of God die out in us? In some lives there may be no external sign of the crisis; but there is an internal crumbling away from all that is pure and holy. That was not the case with Jacob. His full renunciation required a violent struggle with the blazing holiness of God.

The Solicitation of Appeal (32:27–32)

Jacob had to get to the place where he willingly confessed before God the whole guilt of usurping the birthright. This was full and profound and agonizing repentance. The warrior of God is not the man of muscle and a strong jaw, but the man of unutterable weakness, the man who knows he has no power. Jacob was no longer strong in himself; he was strong only in God. His life was no longer marked by striving, but by reliance on God.

You cannot imitate reliance on God. Jacob's wrestling means that he did not want to go through the way he knew he must; he had to come to the end of the best of his natural self, and he struggled in order not to. Then he came to the place where his wisdom was crippled forever. Jacob's limp symbolizes what it looks like in the eyes of shrewd worldly wisdom to cast yourself unperplexed on God.

If you have never been to Peniel, you are sure to come across things that will put your human wisdom into a panic; but if you have seen God face to face, circumstances will no longer arouse any panic in you. We run off on a tangent—anywhere but to Peniel, where we would see God "face to face."

Genesis 33–35

The Still Small Voice

Then God said to Jacob, "Arise, go up to Bethel and dwell there; and make an altar there to God, who appeared to you" (35:1).

On the surface everything seemed right enough to Jacob in Shechem, but underneath everything was wrong. Everything is always wrong when the children of God dwell in Shechem instead of at Bethel. And one day the hollow Shechem peace was shaken by an earthquake—Dinah's fall and her brothers' crime rudely awakened Jacob; then God's voice was heard. It was God unveiling the actuality of sin.

To enter into peace for ourselves without becoming either tolerantly unwatchful of other lives or an amateur providence over them is supremely difficult. God holds us responsible for two things in connection with the lives He brings around us in the apparent haphazard of His providence: insistent waiting on God *for* them and inspired instruction and warning from God *to* them. The thing that astonishes us when we get through to God is the way God holds us responsible for other lives.

The Awakening Voice of God

"Go up to Bethel." This must be the voice of God; no human voice would ever have said what these words imply.

Think what Bethel meant to Jacob: Bethel was the geographical place of God to him. Bethel was the place where the divine promises had been given and vows made, not yet fulfilled. To go back to Bethel meant to acknowledge error.

The voice of God to an awakened soul, when it has heard the voice before, is never to go forward, but to go back. When the blood runs high and impulse worships at the shrine of the heroic, and the nerves strain for the actual doing of something, we not only do not hear God's voice, we don't want to hear it. Then when events have produced an earthquake in the personal life, we find that God was not in the earthquake, but in the still small voice: "Go up to Bethel and dwell there."

The Arousing Virtue of God

Now that Jacob has heard the voice of God speaking to him he is not afraid to assert his authority in his household. When you come across men or women who talk to you from God, you know it by the intuition of your spirit and you obey them, scarcely realizing what you are doing; on looking back you become aware that it was not a human voice at all but the voice of God. Simulated authority should be laughed at, and it is a downright sensible human duty to do so. But when the authority of God comes to you through anyone, to rebel against it would be to rebel against God. But beware of trying to be consistent to the authority that God gives you over any life on a particular occasion; you know that God used you then in that life, yes. But authority never comes from you, but from God through you; therefore let God introduce or withhold as He chooses.

The Appreciated Value of God

Every expansion of heart or brain or spirit must be paid for in added concentration. In the meeting with Esau and the marvelous experience of reconciliation with him, Jacob had an expansion of heart, but he did not pay for it afterward in concentration. He lived loosely in the exalted peace of the expanded life, and suddenly a terrible tragedy breaks up the whole thing.

In our personal lives every expansion of heart, whether it is the awakening of human love or bereavement, must be paid for by watchfulness; if it is not, looseness, ending in moral collapse, is sure to result. Because people do not understand the way they are made, havoc is produced in the lives of those who really have had times with God and have experienced expansions of heart. But they have forgotten to concentrate, and the general feeling of looseness is a sure sign that God's presence has gone.

Jacob settled down in the peace of Shechem, Dinah went to hell, and her brothers to the Devil. Then God spoke to Jacob. If you forget to concentrate on God, the thing that happened in Jacob's domestic life on the big scale will happen in your bodily life on the narrow scale. The vision of what God wants must be paid for by concentration on your part; if it is not, in come the "little foxes," in comes inordinate affection, in come a hundred and one things that were never there before— and down you go. It is not that these things *may* happen; they *will* happen as sure as God is God, unless you watch and pray—that is, unless you concentrate until you are confirmed in the ways of God.

Innocence must be transfigured into virtue by moral choices. We are all apt to be taken in by a frank nature. The man we call frank says of a wrong thing, "I'm sorry I did it," and promptly does it again, and we forgive him, while all the time the deepest devilry goes on. The frank nature brings the glamor of virtue without its reality and stings innocence to death. Innocence is not purity; innocence is right for a child, but criminal for a man or woman. Men and women have no business to be innocent; they ought to be virtuous and pure. Character must be attained.

Individuality, impulse, and innocence are the husk of personal life. Individuality, if it goes beyond a certain point, becomes pig-headedness, determined independence. I have to be prepared to give up my independent right to myself in order that my personality may emerge. Impulse is a subtle snare, always and every time; it may start right, but it is a short-cut to fame or infamy, and it is along the line of impulse that lust and temptation come. Hold back the impulse and you discipline it into character, and it becomes something altogether different—intuition. It is the same with innocence. Innocence must be transformed into purity by a series of moral choices. There is no virtue that has not gone through a moral choice. Yet a great many of us would make virtues out of necessity.

Genesis 37–45

The Boy of God

Joseph, *being* seventeen years old (37:2).

The Bible always incarnates ideals in great personalities, and Joseph stands for the magnificent integrity of boyhood. No man thinks so clearly or has such high ideals as he does in his teens; but unless we live out our ideals, they become a mockery. A man may have fine intellectual views, noble ideals, and his actual life may be beneath contempt, proving that all the high ideals in the world have not the slightest power to bring the life into contact with Reality.

Joseph was amazingly susceptible to God, and he "dreamed dreams." The dreams of the Old Testament are the touch of God on the spirit of a man; but Joseph's brothers did not reverence such dreams. The hatred produced by the sense that another is superior is the most venomous and gives inner meaning to our Lord's words: "They hated Me without a cause."

Beware what you brood on in secret, for the fateful opportunity will come when God and the Devil will meet in your soul, and you will do according to your brooding, swept beyond all control. This is a law as sure as God is God. Beware of saying, "Oh well, it doesn't matter much what I think about in secret." It does, for the time will come when what you think about in secret will find expression in an act. The fateful opportunity came to Joseph's brothers. The Bible always speaks of sin as it appears in its final analysis. Jesus did not say, "You must not covet because it will lead to stealing." He said, "You must not covet because it *is* stealing." He did not say, "You must not be angry with your brother because it will lead to murder." He said, "You must not be angry with your brother because it *is* murder." When the climax of these things is reached, we begin to see the meaning of Calvary.

His Strength Was as the Strength of Ten

A life with presence—that is, an uncommon spirit— redeems any situation from the commonplace. It may be clean- ing boots or doing housework, any ordinary thing at all, but as soon as it is touched by a man or woman with presence it ceases to be commonplace. The rarest asset to a godly life is to be practically conscientious in every situation: "But the LORD was with Joseph . . . and He gave him favor in the sight of the keeper of the prison."

Joseph's adaptability was superb. Adaptability is not tact. Tact is frequently nothing but the moral counterpart of hypoc- risy. Adaptability is the power to make a suitable environment for oneself out of any set of circumstances. Most of us are all right if we can live in our own particular setting, with our own crowd, but when we get pitchforked somewhere else, either we cannot adapt ourselves, or we adapt ourselves too easily and lose God. Joseph did not lose God. God was with Joseph in Egypt as He had been in Canaan; He was with him in the prison as He was in the house of his master.

If we simply delight in a godly atmosphere and refuse to appropriate God for ourselves, when we have to leave the godly atmosphere we will find ourselves God-less. Then our natural adaptability becomes the adaptability to degenerate.

Complete Steel

The phrase "complete steel" is Milton's definition of chastity, and is peculiarly appropriate to Joseph. Personal chastity is an impregnable barrier against evil. Like virtue, chastity is not a gift, but an attainment of determined integrity. Unsoiledness may be nothing more than necessity, the result of a shielded life, and is no more chastity than innocence is purity. Virtue and chastity are forged by us, not by God. You can't drown a cork, and you can't defile Joseph.

Four times over in this chapter is the statement made, "the Lord was with Joseph." It is the presence of God that is the secret of victory always. The fear of the Lord creates an atmosphere in which impure thoughts and unholy desires die a natural death. Joseph knew that the God whom he worshiped "could not look on iniquity." The outstanding value of the Bible is that it makes shameful things appear shameful because it never analyzes them. The discovery of the desperate recesses in the human heart is the greatest evidence of the need for redemption. The experiences of life awaken possibilities of evil that make us shudder, and as long as we remain under the refuge of innocence we are fools. The appalling things revealed in human lives confirm the words of the great Master of the human heart. Our Lord did not say, "into the heart of man these things are injected"; He said, "from within, out of the heart of man, proceed . . ." and then follows the terrible catalogue. We ought to get into the habit of measuring ourselves by this rugged standard. The important thing to remember is that we are to trust the revelations of Jesus Christ, not our own innocence. The only thing that safeguards is the Redemption.

Joseph's high vocation was to preserve life. God brings His purposes to pass in spite of all men may do, and often through what they do. He will use the very things that look as if they are going dead against such fulfillment. God goes steadily on and involves us in the fulfillment.

"*It was* not you *who* sent me here, but God. . . . You meant evil against me; *but* God meant it for good" (45:8; 50:20).

Note to the Reader

The publisher invites you to share your response to the message of this book by writing Discovery House Publishers, P.O. Box 3566, Grand Rapids, MI 49501 U.S.A. or by calling 800-283-8333. For information about other Discovery House publications, contact us at the same address and phone number.